I Can't Turn Back

I Can't Turn Back

A Journey from Spiritual Displacement to Divine Redemption.

Shabriya Hill

I Can't Turn Back: A Journey from

Spiritual Displacement to Divine Redemption
Copyright © 2025 by Shabriya Hill

Shabriya.HillO@gmail.com

ISBN: 9798991278331
Library of Congress Control Number: 2025907359
(Paperback)

This book contains stories from the author's life. In some cases, names, identifying details, and event timelines have been changed to protect the privacy of individuals involved.

Printed in the United States of America.

Publisher: On a Hill Publishing co.

First Edition

Dedication

For Ka'Mya,

My beautiful daughter, my reason to keep fighting. When darkness threatened to consume me, your face was the light that guided me home. Your existence saved me in more ways than you'll ever know.

For the God who never gave up on me,

Even when I gave up on myself. You pursued me through hospital rooms and wrong decisions, through broken relationships and shattered dreams. This story belongs to you—every page a testament to your relentless grace.

Epigraph

"I have blotted out your transgressions like a cloud and your sins like mist; return to me, for I have redeemed you."

Isaiah 44:22 ESV

Book Structure Outline

Front Matter

Main Content

Preface

I wrote this book to share joy.

Joy is a profound, enduring state of well-being and contentment, a fruit of the Holy Spirit, rather than a fleeting emotion, stemming from faith in God and His promises, even amidst trials.

I never understood what it was to have joy before submitting to God; I never knew peace until I walked with Jesus.

I pray you discover hope within these pages. I pray that by sharing my testimony and revealing how God has moved in my life, that you will raise your faith and expectations for His movement in yours. I can't turn back; is more than a declaration. It is the much-needed rest after decades of being lost, wandering through the wilderness, and choosing death every day. It is my rejoice when Christ showed me life was an option, that I didn't have to continue living to die, when I could be dying to live. As I live out the words in this book, I'm still learning new ways to crucify my flesh daily. It is not always easy. While writing, I can't turn back; I did not want to relive a lot of my past trauma and experiences. On top of that, having lost a lot of memories due to my stroke, they were now all racing back to the forefront of my mind, now more vivid than ever. After running to God in prayer, I fell on my face and admitted, "Abba, I don't know if I can do this." I can't turn back became my plea. Yes, I knew he was capable. Yes, I believe He is working all things out for my good. And at the same time, I knew I could not do this. Coming face-to face with all the pain and trauma that kept me in bondage for so long seemed like a threat to my journey and the peace He provided. I can't turn back, is a constant reminder of how God is made strong in our weakness, I can do all things through Christ who strengthens me, and most importantly, this is not a story about Shabriya, but a testimony about the God that has gotten me through. How the creator of all life stands with his creation side by side, every step of the way. A witness of the Alpha and the Omega, and all the times His strength shone through my weakest moments. A good God helped me to navigate what I thought was a story about pain and trauma, and allowed me to see the truth, that my testimony was one about Grace and redemption through Christ Jesus and how God will never forsaken or abandons us.

I can't turn back is about a God who loves us so much that he sacrificed his only begotten son, who died on the cross for our sins and rose three days later so that we may have eternal life.

Navigating pain, trauma, and disappointment is not "a walk in the park," but Jesus gives us victory ahead of the journey. Offering us redemption ahead of transformation. Offering to save us from sin and its consequences before we even think about becoming more like Him.

Coming to Christ and choosing to live with Him has given me freedom and peace that would be too selfish to keep hidden.

News too good not to share.

He is deserving of all the glory, honor, and praise. If you can see how God has stood by me, hopefully it will reveal how he continues to stand with you, waiting for you to call "ABBA, I need you."

I pray this story helps you realize that you also can't turn back.

-   Shabriya Hill- Okumbele

OUR TESTIMONY OF GOD'S GRACE AND DELIVER-ANCE OVER OUR LIVES IS A powerful weapon AGAINST THE DEVIL"

-   Crystal McDowell

Chapter 1

Genesis

From the Harlem of the West

"From one man he made all the nations, that
they should inhabit the whole earth; and he
marked out their appointed times in history
and the boundaries of their lands." (Acts
17:26)

In San Francisco, less than a mile from what would later become the headquarters of some of the biggest tech companies and homes to some of the wealthiest people in America, yet separated by an invisible gulf wider than any ocean, I grew up a young girl in the Fillmore district. This area, once known as the Harlem of the West, was once thriving with Black people, Black businesses, Black music, and Black culture.

Though I was born too late to witness this golden era, I lived amid its fading echoes and ruins. Like many of us who inhabited it, the neighborhood was spiritually displaced—a community that remembered what it once was but struggled to maintain its identity against forces determined to erase it. Looking back, I can see how this mirrored my spiritual disconnection and eventual rediscovery journey.

Just as Fillmore had lost its vibrant spiritual center—the thriving churches and faith-based connections that once anchored the community—I, too, would wander through my early life spiritually adrift, searching for something I couldn't name. The Scripture says, 'The boundary lines have fallen for me in pleasant places' (Psalm 16:6), but neither I nor my neighborhood could recognize the pleasant places amid our shared desolation.

Within those few square blocks, however, God was writing parallel stories of redemption—one for a community striving to reclaim its soul, and another for a young girl who would eventually find her way back to faith after years of wandering. The spiritual disorientation I experienced growing up in a neighborhood that had lost its way oddly prepared me to recognize the profound relief of returning home to God years later.

Beginnings in Fillmore

World War II brought an influx of black people from all over the South seeking opportunities to work in the shipyards. Most of them settled in the Fillmore, and my great-grandparents were no exception. Each block of the Fillmore was filled with Black homeowners and Black entertainment. Black-owned markets, doctors' and dentists' offices, shoe and apparel stores, barbershops, gas stations, auto garages, salons, and nightclubs created a Mecca of Black culture and entertainment in the Fillmore. By the 1970s, however, most of the businesses had been wiped out as the Fillmore experienced heavy gentrification, except for a few low-income housing projects that had crammed the remaining Black residents in. My parents watched family and friends leave and their grandparents' homes sold off as they remained in Fillmore through the gentrification.

By the time I was born, Fillmore was a shadow of its former self. Very few Black businesses remained, and our neighborhoods, once filled with glory, were now overrun with alcohol, drugs, and guns. The Harlem of the West was officially gone, now merely a story of how amazing it once was. I did experience the community that was left behind— one that survived its attempted erasure. It had transformed and rebuilt itself, possessing a unique beauty that I treasured deeply. We built a tight knit village with what was left behind, filled with friends and family I saw every day, everyone knew each other, even the store owners knew my parents and grandparents, and would call us by name. Reminding us that our parents were only a phone call away, if we even thought about acting out.

The Roots of Faith and Family

"A father to the fatherless, a defender of widows, is God in his holy dwelling." (Psalm 68:5)

"Lil Mac Chewy, is that you?" Mac Chewy was the name the streets had given my father. I beamed with joy at the mention of the name of the man I never had the chance to know. "Lil Mac Chewy, is that you?" "Girl, you look just like your daddy."

Each encounter was both a gift and a wound—confirmation that I belonged to someone important enough to be remembered, yet painful reminders of an absence that shaped our family in countless ways. I collected these fragments of my father like precious stones, storing them away as part of my identity. Years later, when I would struggle to understand God as a Father who would never leave or forsake me, these early experiences would both complicate and eventually deepen my faith journey. The Scripture says that God is "a father to the fatherless" (Psalm 68:5) but embracing that truth would require healing from the earthly example that had been taken from me so early.

Being recognized as his daughter meant I could expect a couple of dollars or, if we were at the corner store, a "grab what you want" would be my cue to fill my hands with chips and 10-cent candies. "Thank you", I smiled as I skipped away.

Skipping past the used needles, drug addicts, and empty liquor bottles to enter the pee-stained elevator and pinching my nose until we got off on the floor of my godmother's apartment was the beginning of a fun Saturday afternoon spent playing with my siblings and our god-brothers.

> *"And my God will meet all your needs according to the riches of his glory in Christ Jesus."* (Philippians 4:19)

I never realized we were so poor. In my child's mind, we had everything essential: food (most days), shelter (of varying forms), and most importantly, each other. We were having too much fun to be struggling—or so I thought. My mother's creative spirit always transformed our circumstances into adventures.

"We're going camping tonight!" she would announce with forced enthusiasm on nights when we had nowhere else to go. Our car became our bedroom, and the parking lot our temporary address. My mom would drive around the city streets all night, pointing out landmarks as though we were tourists rather than homeless. The drive-in movie theater became our favorite destination—where our living situation seemed intentional rather than desperate.

We would often go to the drive-in movies; that was my favorite. And even today, I must admit, I still love drive-in movies. I don't mind traveling the extra distance to find a now-rare gem.

"Get in the trunk," my mom would instruct as we approached the ticketing window—an odd directive I never questioned, too excited about the movies and snacks ahead. The prospect of staying up watching films under the stars and munching on treats until sleep overtook us filled me with childlike joy. It wasn't until I was much older that I realized this trunk-hiding was my mother's strategy to avoid paying for my admission because she could only afford one ticket. I simply believed my mom was just adventurous and fun-loving. Her encouragement to stay out late and our constant driving around the city seemed normal, it was all a part of her game we played. Since we spent so much time at my grandmothers' houses, I assumed we lived there with them or split our time between both places, unaware of our actual housing insecurity.

There's profound spiritual truth in Christ's words that "blessed are the poor in spirit, for theirs is the kingdom of heaven" (Matthew 5:3). Without knowing it, I was learning early lessons about finding joy independent of circumstances and identifying blessings amid hardship— spiritual muscles that would later serve me well in my faith journey. What seemed like childhood resilience was God's provision of a specific strength I would need throughout my life.

> *"The LORD is close to the brokenhearted and saves those who are crushed in spirit."*
> *(Psalm 34:18)*

I experienced my first loss at two years old, and it has weighed heavily on me for thirty-one years.

My father's death wasn't just the loss of a person but the collapse of our family's entire ecosystem. When he died, the very concept of "happy family" died with him, replaced by something fractured and unfamiliar. The village that had once surrounded us scattered like leaves in the wind, leaving my mother to face her grief in isolation.

Scripture tells us, "The LORD is close to the brokenhearted and saves those who are crushed in spirit" (Psalm 34:18), but this truth remained hidden from me for decades.

Instead, that early loss instilled in me a subconscious expectation that good things—especially people— eventually disappear. This weight followed me for thirtyone years, coloring my relationships, my self-worth, and especially my ability to trust in God's consistent presence.

Looking back through the eyes of faith, I can see that God was present even then, preserving my life and spirit through that devastating time. Though my mother's depression created another kind of absence in our home, God was weaving a redemption story that would eventually transform even this deepest wound into something that could help others heal.

We were often left with our aunts and cousins while she grappled with how to cope. She struggled for months, then years, with her grief. She had just lost her husband, the love of her life, her protector, her provider, and the father of her children. She had no idea what to do next.

One day, we returned to my grandmother's house to find the locks had been changed. That pivotal moment marked the beginning of our homelessness, though at four years old, with my sister only two—I was too young to grasp how dire our situation truly was. My mother, suddenly without shelter for her children, kept her pain hidden from us as we moved from couch to couch, she transformed

these nights into adventures, trying to make our circumstances seem normal. Most days, she went hungry so we
wouldn't have to, though sometimes there wasn't enough for
us. Through it all, she never showed emotion, never complained, and was too proud to ask for help. She persevered,
shielding us from the harsh reality that we no longer had a
home to return to.

> ***"My grace is sufficient for you, for my power***
> ***is made perfect in weakness."*** *(2 Corinthians*
> *12:9)*

My mother was my superhero; she had never allowed us to
see her hurt. I had never even seen her cry. So why now?
Who hurt her?

I woke up from what I thought was sleep. I was tired. My
throat was sore and felt uncomfortable, as though I needed
to cough but could not. My head felt heavy, but I felt no
pain. I heard soft sniffles and saw my mom crying quietly
in the corner. A large man was consoling her, hugging her
so tightly that I couldn't see his face. I tried to get their
attention, but she just kept crying. I attempted to talk, but
no words came out. I cleared my throat and tried yelling as
loud as I could.

"Mom! What's wrong?" she continued to cry, her head
hanging low. "Mom... Mom!" I screamed, but she didn't
budge. I thought something must be wrong; what was
going on? I had never seen my mom cry. Through all she
had endured, I had watched her struggle, fight, and prevail,
but never had I witnessed her weep. Panic set in. I wanted
her to know I was okay, I decided to get up since I couldn't
speak. I turned to the side of the bed and used all my

strength to lift myself and walk over to my mom, trying to gain her attention. But the man stood in the way.

Annoyance washed over me. Who was this man? What the hell had he done to my mom? Anger was building inside me, ready to burst from every pore, primed to fight and protect her. A tempest of emotions swirled within me. My eyes quickly scanned the room, searching for answers. The man embraced her, crying in unison. Who is this? I yelled.

There was something familiar about him. "Mom!" I yelled again. She wouldn't respond or even move. It was like I hadn't been speaking, yet I was screaming at the top of my lungs. "Hello!!" Nothing I said or did would provoke a response from her. She didn't even flinch; she just sat there, crying incessantly. "WAIT! WHY AM I IN THE HOSPITAL? WHAT HAPPENED?"

I was overwhelmed with questions, and no one was there to provide answers. Her tears consumed her, so she didn't even notice I was standing there. I decided to speak to the man. "Excuse me, sir? Sir. Hi, can you hear me?" He did not move. "HELLO!" His only response was to hug my mom tighter.

Okay, I understand, but if she could see me, she might stop crying! He began to whisper to my mom, "It's alright; she's going to be alright." "I've got her… sniff… I've got her." "Who? Hello? Who are you? What? You got who? Who is h... Dad? DAD!? DAD!! " I screamed through tears. Could he see me? Could my mom see him? He never diverted his attention from my mom, not even to me. Am I seeing a ghost? I wondered to myself. Am I losing my mind? I suddenly started to feel light-headed. I need to sit down.

I stumbled back towards the bed. As I approached, I noticed someone was already in it. I looked down in horror to see myself. Hot tears fell from my eyes as I examined my body. "Oh, Shabriya, what happened to you? " My head was shaved, gauze wrapped around, protecting the bloodstained bandages. Something was sticking out of the front of my head. It looked like it had gone into my skull— something I'd never seen before. I looked down at my neck. There was a hole in my neck, something holding it open. Tubes down my nose, and IVs with multiple tubes in my arm. Even with all that was going on my swollen face looked as if I were sleeping peacefully.

I couldn't believe it. The thought choked me up. Did I... did I die? I said to myself. No, no, no, no. What happened?

Stunned, I sat in disbelief, trying to process how I got here. What happened, I couldn't remember. Something was wrong—. My last clear memory was a sudden, searing pain exploding through my head, followed by darkness washing over me like a tide. Voices swirled around me, urgent and afraid. Shayla's voice cut through the fog, calling my name from what seemed miles away.

"Shabriya! SHABRIYA!"

I wanted to respond, to reassure her, but my body refused to obey the simplest commands. The gap between my thoughts and my physical form had become an uncrossable chasm. In those final moments before they wheeled me away, I poured every ounce of will into moving just one finger—a sign, any sign, that I was still present. A sign, that I hadn't completely slipped away.

I prayed then, not with practiced words but with desperate need. "God, please, let me move enough for them to know I'm here."

Whether it was divine intervention or some final spark of connection between brain and body, something shifted. Shayla's voice rose excitedly, but a clinical voice quickly dismissed the movement as involuntary. As consciousness faded and the anesthesia pulled me under, I felt myself slipping into a place between worlds—a realm neither fully here nor fully beyond.

What followed was unlike anything I could have prepared for—the boundaries between reality, dreams, and something altogether different blurred. I existed outside my body, looking down at the shell that had once contained me. I tried to rejoin it, to slip back inside like putting on a familiar coat, but something fundamental had changed.

"God, am I dead?" I called into the vast emptiness, feeling a presence, I couldn't see but somehow recognized.

The full details of what happened next—the visitors, the journeys, the revelations about my soul and salvation— would forever alter how I understood life, death, and everything that matters in between. But before any of that...

He took me back to the beginning.

Chapter 2

Foundations

Lesson from Mother's Pew

"Train up a child in the way he should go;
even when he is old, he will not depart from
it." (Proverbs 22:6)

"Sundays are for church." Church was our time. Every
Saturday, I would stay with my great-aunt and great-
grandmother. I loved going over there; I was treated like a
princess. My great-aunt Virginia would do my hair however I wanted (mostly in spiral curls) and cook me The most
delicious food!

"There's nothing to eat?" I said, annoyed, holding the
refrigerator open. "I'm starving!" I yelled dramatically. "I
haven't eaten all day!"

I watched as she rummaged through the cabinets, interrupting every few minutes, only to tell her what I didn't want.
"Hush," she shot back, giving me a sharp look that unmis-
takably communicated I was crossing a line. The tension in
the air thickened. My cue to do as I was told.

I went to sit at the dining room table directly across from
the kitchen. I pulled out the chair covered in plastic and sat
at the table, decorated for "special occasions" and the occasional "special guest." I flipped through old magazines until
I heard the fire crackling and grease popping. As the garlic
and onion filled the air, I called her again, "Mmm, Auntie,
that smells good! What's in it?" I asked excitedly. "Just a
little something I threw together," she replied with a smile.
Some of the best meals I've ever had, came out of that tiny
kitchen from my auntie.

My aunt was a great cook; she could make anything. Those weekends, sitting in the kitchen while she cooked, and we talked and laughed, sparked my interest in cooking. Watching her whip up an entire meal from the same seemingly empty cabinets I had just searched was like magic. I was inspired, and it would later fuel my desire to start my own food business.

As a child, I was fortunate to be close to my greatgrandmother. She was the mother I felt I didn't have at home, the woman I aspired to become one day. Unlike the chaotic unpredictability I experienced elsewhere, Mother provided steady, intentional guidance filled with extraordinary kindness. Her gentle nature wrapped around me like a protective blanket whenever I visited. She taught me to be a lady, not through lessons on posture and polite conversation but by demonstrating dignity rooted in something deeper than appearance.

"Prayer isn't just for church, baby," she would tell me while washing dishes, her voice soft but certain. She showed me how daily tasks could become moments of communion with God. She taught me to start my day with "Good morning, Lord" and end with gratitude before sleep. When I faced childhood disappointments or felt uncertain about myself, she didn't just offer empty comfort. She opened her worn Bible, reading passages until I understood that my worth came from being cherished by God.

These weren't merely religious rituals—Mother showed me through her consistent kindness that a relationship with God meant experiencing His tenderness in everyday moments. The way she listened attentively when I spoke, her patience when teaching me to cook, and her gentle corrections when I misbehaved all demonstrated how divine love could flow through human hands. Through her example, I learned to look for God's hand in both struggles and joys and to recognize kindness as the most genuine expression of faith.

Lula Mae Johnson, affectionately known as Mother, was a vision of graceful dignity—beautiful, smart, sweet, and feminine. Though short in stature with fair skin, she carried herself with the presence of royalty. Her smile possessed a rare quality, illuminating any room she entered with genuine warmth that made everyone feel special, especially a little girl starved for attention.

Unlike my own mother, whose beauty was often hidden behind closed doors and expressions of pain, Mother adorned herself as if each day were a celebration of life itself. She was always dressed elegantly—furs draped over her shoulders, jewelry that caught the light, meticulously coordinated outfits, and those magnificent hats and wigs! She was always decked out, especially for church.

Where other women in my neighborhood dressed for survival, whether to fit in with the crowd or fade into the background, Mother dressed to honor herself and her God. The women I saw daily moved through life with shoulders weighed down by burdens; their femininity was sometimes lost to hardship. My own mother's beauty had become obscured by grief and struggle after my father's death.

But Mother showed me another way to exist as a woman—one where dignity wasn't surrendered to circumstances. Her appearance wasn't about vanity but about self-respect and reverence. When she prepared for church, it was an act of worship itself. "We present our best to the Lord," she'd say while securing her hat with a pearl-tipped pin, teaching me that how we present ourselves can be a form of devotion.

In a world where the women around me seemed defined by what they lacked or had lost, Mother defined herself by what she chose to embody—grace, strength, faith, and beauty that radiated from her spirit and appearance. This wasn't just about clothes but refusing to let hardship diminish your light. It was a lesson I would need desperately in the years to come.

The Inheritance of Faith

"Jesus said to her, 'I am the resurrection and the life. Whoever believes in me, though he dies, yet shall he live.'" (John 11:25)

Mother was dressed to the nines in all white, wearing her fanciest hat. "We need to go," she said, rushing toward the door. I was ready; my aunt had just curled my hair to perfection. I wore the prettiest blue floral dress, new stockings with frills, and shiny new white dress shoes. I felt beautiful in a way that transcended the new dress and carefully curled hair. For a child who often felt invisible or burdensome at home, being the focus of such loving attention felt like glimpsing a different version of myself— one worthy of care and celebration. I had woken before sunrise, too excited to sleep, my stomach fluttering with the same anticipation I felt on Christmas mornings.

"Easter is even more important than Christmas," Mother had explained while preparing my outfit the night before. Christmas gave us the baby Jesus, but Easter gave us our salvation." Though I couldn't articulate the theological significance then, I understood somehow that this day was of great importance. The special clothes, the extra preparation, and Mother's joy signaled that we were participating in something sacred. We weren't just dressed for church but adorned to honor a miracle.

Sunday Mornings and Sacred Teachings

"Let us not neglect our meeting together, as some people do, but encourage one another, especially now that the day of his return is drawing near." (Hebrews 10:25)

We always left early on Sundays, rising before the sun painted the sky. Mother insisted on punctuality as a form of reverence—"God's always on time," she'd say, "and so should we be." The journey to church required patience; we had a long bus ride ahead, transferring once and sometimes walking several blocks when buses ran late.

During spring, our early mornings were shrouded in San Francisco's infamous fog, the air damp and crispy cold against my skin. I'd huddle close to Mother, her warmth a shield against the morning chill. The weather was often harsh enough to justify staying home, but such thoughts never crossed Mother's mind. Rain or shine, fog or clear skies, she maintained an unwavering commitment to worship.

"Weather is just weather," she'd tell me when I complained about the cold. "But the Word of God is eternal." It was my first lesson in prioritizing spiritual nourishment over physical comfort. Nothing—fog, distance, or early hours—deterred Mother from arriving on time for Bible study and staying for the full Sunday service. While other adults might skip church for lesser inconveniences, Mother demonstrated that true faith required showing up consistently, regardless of circumstances.

I didn't realize then that I was witnessing more than just church attendance—I was observing spiritual discipline. Mother's steadfast devotion planted seeds that would grow into my understanding of faithfulness. Long before I could articulate what commitment to God meant, I saw it lived out in those cold morning bus rides, her determined steps toward the church doors, and her refusal to let temporary discomfort interfere with eternal matters.

Once we arrived, I enjoyed the activities and the donuts, so I didn't mind being there early. On Easter, we learned about my favorite Bible story—the empty tomb and risen Christ. Even at that early age, I felt surprisingly happy and confident learning that Jesus had conquered death. The story resonated with something deep inside me, though I lacked the spiritual vocabulary to express why. I didn't understand its theological importance or personal implications at the time. All the adults seemed overjoyed, so I mirrored their celebration, clapping to the triumphant hymns.

Looking back now, I realize God was planting seeds of resurrection hope that would lie dormant for decades before fully blooming. What I absorbed as a simple happy ending—Jesus didn't stay dead!—would later become my lifeline during my own brush with death. The resurrection story that once merely entertained me as a child would eventually become the foundation of my faith—the assurance that God brings life from death, purpose from pain, and dawn after the darkest nights. Though I couldn't comprehend it then, those early Easter celebrations prepared my heart to recognize God's resurrection power when I needed it most.

It was Easter Sunday, and the church was packed. All the ladies had on fancy dresses and big hats. I loved those big fancy hats! Mother wouldn't let me play with hers, but I would sneak moments to try it on, when she wasn't looking. After Bible study, I ran through the halls and into the church for service. Mother sang in the choir, so I would sit with the other kids during service, humming hymns and judging who had the best and worst hat. From my spot in the pew, I'd watch her stand tall among the other singers, her face transformed with an expression I rarely saw elsewhere— pure joy. Even when we faced struggles at home, Mother's countenance in that choir stand radiated peace.

I noticed how she closed her eyes during certain parts of songs, as though the music carried her somewhere beyond that small church building. Other choir members might flip through papers or glance at the congregation, but Mother sang as if she and God were having a private conversation through the music.

"Your great-grandmother doesn't just sing," an elderly church member once told me. "She ministers." I didn't fully understand what that meant then, but I sensed it was true. Her service wasn't about performance—it was an offering.

Years later, when I faced my crossroads of faith, I remembered Mother in that choir stand. Her commitment to serving through music taught me that worship wasn't just something you attended but participated in with your whole heart. It showed me that using your gifts for God's glory brings a fulfillment that nothing else can match. Though

I never inherited her singing voice, I did inherit her understanding that serving God's people is not a burden but a privilege—a lesson that would sustain me through my darkest moments.

I was ready to go after what felt like forever.

Listening to the pastor preach, praying and singing, watching the ladies get carried out after catching the Holy Ghost, and observing people talk in tongues. I was bored... most of us kids were, so we started cracking jokes and playing around. We whispered and laughed as the elders spoke in tongues and were carried out, their bodies seemingly overtaken by some invisible force. The children's section would erupt in muffled giggles when someone would "catch the Holy Ghost" and run down the aisle, arms waving, feet barely touching the ground. At the time, I didn't understand—I thought it was all a show, an elaborate performance that adults put on because it was expected in church.

"What's wrong with her?" I'd whisper to my friend, watching an usher fan a woman whose body trembled while tears streamed down her face.

"She got the Holy Ghost," came the knowing reply, though I doubted my friend understood better than I did.

I couldn't fathom why anyone would want to lose control like that, to become so vulnerable in front of others. In my young mind, strength meant keeping your emotions tightly contained—a lesson I'd learned watching my mother soldier through her pain after my father died. These displays seemed foreign, even frightening.

Years later, after my encounter with God during my hospital stay, I understood what I had witnessed in those pews. What I had dismissed as theatrical, was surrender— souls so filled with the presence of God that physical bodies could no longer contain the experience. What looked like a loss of control was the highest form of liberation, allowing the Spirit to move without the constraints of human dignity or social expectations.

When I eventually experienced the Holy Spirit's presence myself—feeling that overwhelming wave of divine love wash over me, bringing tears, trembling, and indescribable joy—I finally understood what those church elders had been experiencing all along. It wasn't a performance but a profound connection. The Holy Spirit wasn't something they "caught" like a contagion but Someone they had an intimate relationship with, a Divine Presence they had welcomed so completely into their hearts that it overflowed into physical expression.

This intimate communion with the Holy Spirit became something I yearned for, something I had unknowingly been searching for even as a child, watching those expressions of worship with confusion. I realized that my soul had been created for what I had been witnessing— direct, unfiltered communion with God, transcending intellectual understanding or social propriety.

I realized then how much I had missed as a child, how I had been witnessing genuine communion with God, but lacked the spiritual eyes to see it. Those elders weren't performing; they were experiencing a heavenly touch that transcended human understanding. The very manifestations I had mocked became the experiences I would long for—

moments when God's presence became so real that self consciousness dissolved in the face of a divine encounter.

When Scripture speaks of being "filled with the Spirit," I think of those Sunday mornings in that small church, where faithful believers had no concern for appearances when the Spirit of God moved among them. Their example taught me that authentic worship isn't always dignified or contained— sometimes, it breaks free of our careful boundaries, just as God's love breaks through our carefully constructed walls.

While I was having a ball laughing with the other kids in the pews, I looked up to the choir seats and caught a glare from Mother so intense that I immediately stopped playing and straightened up. She didn't stop singing, just looked at me, and I didn't want to test my luck or her patience. After spending all day at church, or at least most of it, we finally headed to my grandmother's house. My stomach was empty by then, and I couldn't wait for the Easter meal.

Chapter 3

Planting Seeds

Words That Shaped a Life

"For whatever one sows, that will he also reap." (Galatians 6:7)

The bright, brave, and courageous child I was, had disappeared before middle school ended.

Mother, who was once my safe place, my role model, and my guidance, had become very ill. Suffering from dementia and Alzheimer's. The woman who guided me could no longer even remember who I was. The support and spiritual guidance were gone, and I was left to figure things out on my own.

"Carry each other's burdens, and in this way you will fulfill the law of Christ." (Galatians 6:2)

In my 7th-grade year, I made a decision that would alter not just my education but my spiritual formation. I told my mom it was okay to take me out of my private Catholic school and put me into public school with my siblings. "I just want to try something different," I explained to her and the dean with practiced casualness, as though changing schools was a simple preference rather than a sacrifice.

I had been watching my mother's face grow more strained each month. Despite her silence about financial matters, the weight of her burden was evident in her increasing physical and emotional absences. She was struggling, laid off from her job, and searching for something new for months. Things weren't the same at home anymore. Though she was physically present more often, confined to her bedroom with the door firmly shut, she had never been more distant from us.

My daily religion classes taught me about sacrifice and carrying one another's burdens. "Carry each other's burdens, and in this way, you will fulfill the law of Christ," my teacher had quoted from Scripture. Perhaps this was my chance to live that teaching, though I couldn't articulate it so clearly then. What I knew was that I could be the one to ease her struggle, rather than wait for her to tell me she couldn't afford my education anymore.

In reality, I was starting to feel embarrassed about being constantly pulled out of class in the middle of instruction. They didn't announce it publicly, but we all knew what that meant: she couldn't pay my tuition. The whispers grew, as I headed to the principal's office. They spoke to me about how far behind I was, as if the tuition was my responsibility. I was constantly threatened with being sent home and unable to return if the balance wasn't met. They poked and prodded for answers about what was happening at home. I opened my mouth to speak when I suddenly remembered my mom's voice: "What happens in this house stays in this house! " "Nothing", I answered softly. They continued with a series of unanswered phone calls to my mother.

At 12, I had already begun to reason through my mother's adult problems and took them on as my own. I overheard my mother complaining about my sister entering middle school and how worried she was that she couldn't afford to send us both to Catholic school.

"She could barely afford to send me", I thought to myself. Well, not comfortably, anyway. Maybe she wouldn't be so sad if she didn't have to pay for my schooling and spend so much on me. I would be with my sister and cousins again, which would be a win-win situation. Or so I thought.

I wanted to relieve my mom of that burden. Since it was technically my decision, she wouldn't need to feel guilty about telling me I couldn't go.

I had been telling my teachers I wouldn't be returning the next school year, and the principal immediately wanted to meet with my mom and me.

"They may need to remove me officially. I don't know. " I responded to my mom after she questioned what the meeting was about. Imagine my surprise when the principal said they would waive my tuition, allowing me to attend for free. I glanced at my mom, whose expression remained unchanged. "No," I responded. "I'll be going to a public High School anyway, so I should just get used to it," I said, hoping my mom would step in. The principal began discussing all the scholarships available and how I could attend High School for free.

Attending a private school in San Francisco, while my mom was struggling and my siblings were in public school, did not make sense to me. I didn't believe it was possible, definitely not anything I deserved.

"No, thank you," I replied, instantly regretting my decision. I convinced myself that I didn't want to be in high school with all those rich kids anyway. The principal continued, saying I was a bright student who could have a real future.

My mind wandered as she spoke, attempting to ignore her lies. If they could afford to let me attend for free, what was the point of pulling me out of class in front of everyone? Why not mention this earlier?

No thanks, I said once again for the final time.

"The words of the reckless pierce like swords, but the tongue of the wise brings healing."
(Proverbs 12:18)

Growing up as the eldest daughter of a black widowed woman, now a single mother. Meant I was now the second parent. My mom was busy trying to navigate her trauma and depression while unintentionally starting my own.

The atmosphere in our home transformed gradually, then suddenly, like twilight shifting to darkness while you're distracted. My mother, once my fiercest protector, began to view me differently. Perhaps it was my developing body that reminded her I wasn't her baby anymore, or maybe my growing independence threatened her. Whatever the cause, everything that went wrong became my responsibility—from my siblings' homework to the household bills she'd complain about...

"You need to step up," she'd say, as though childhood were a luxury I'd overstayed.

Her expressions of anger took new, cutting forms. What began as occasional sharp comments evolved into a steady stream of verbal wounds.

"You ain't they mama!" she'd snap as I struggled to get my siblings to listen, as she prepared to leave and told me to watch them.

"You think you're so smart, but you ain't all that," she'd argue when I'd offer solutions to household problems, dismissing my intelligence even as she expected me to handle adult responsibilities.

"Mac nasty," she'd call me, a cruel twist on my father's nickname that once felt like affection.

Each name, criticism, and dismissal planted seeds in the fertile soil of my adolescent self-image. And like any seed given consistent attention—even negative attention—they began to grow, putting down roots in my sense of identity and worth.

I was so hurt that I would spend days in my room, crying and writing about it. I couldn't understand how I went from being loved and supported to someone she hated. That shift was hard to navigate, and I had to hide how I felt about it. I didn't want anyone to think I was "soft" I wouldn't dare show any vulnerability because then it would be used to hurt me all the time. Her words were like daggers to my self-esteem.

B**ch! Ugly, fat, dumb, mac nasty. They were some of her favorites. Slowly but surely, I started to believe every word, and it didn't help that acne had taken over my once baby smooth face.

I had become deeply sad, as the seeds she sowed had begun to take root.

The Slow Growth of Pain

> *"For God has not given us a spirit of fear, but of power and of love and of a sound mind."* (2 Timothy 1:7)

The transformation was subtle—almost unnoticeable to others, perhaps, but greatly felt within me. The outgoing child who once raced through church hallways and commanded attention in class discussions retreated into shadows, preferring the safety of isolation to the risks of visibility.

While my sister and brother played outside, navigating the neighborhood with the resilience of children, I created a different world inside. AOL chat rooms became my sanctuary—digital spaces where nobody could see my acne-marked face or judge my changing body. Online, I crafted a version of myself unburdened by my mother's criticisms or classmates' judgments. Nobody there knew I was "ugly," "fat," or "Mac nasty." They only knew the words I typed and the thoughts I chose to share.

I convinced myself this was protection—if no one saw me, no one could hurt me. Yet even then, something inside me recognized the danger in this retreat. The God I'd learned about in Catholic school was not a God of isolation but of community. Mother had shown me that faith flourishes

in connection with others. But my great-grandmother had fallen ill, removing the one spiritual anchor I had depended on. Without her gentle guidance and consistent kindness, I felt spiritually adrift, with no compass to navigate my growing pain.

In my isolation, I chose separation over vulnerability, building digital walls that kept others out while keeping me trapped within. I couldn't see then how isolation, while feeling like safety, was fertile ground for those negative seeds to grow unchallenged. Without the counterbalance of other perspectives, my mother's words became my inner voice, and the identity she assigned me became the only one I knew.

I started to write songs and poetry as an outlet to release some of the pain I was experiencing. I wrote about everything and read everything often, wishing to be whisked far away from home and from my mother.

In reality, I was here helping with her kids. I ensured they were dressed and ready for school every morning, walked them to and from home, fed them, babysat them all the time, and cared for my baby sister, who was 10 years younger. When my sister was born, I felt I finally had someone to love me back. I promised to show her the love my mom could not give. I decided to fill in the gaps, becoming more of a mother figure than a sister. I would spend the rest of my childhood standing in for my mom. Most times, because I had no choice, I was determined to make sure she would never feel the way I did.

> *"You shall know the truth, and the truth shall make you free."* (John 8:32)

Looking back with the clarity that only time and healing can provide, I see my mother differently now. Behind her harsh words and emotional absence was a woman drowning in her undiagnosed mental health issues and unprocessed trauma. Carrying unhealed wounds from her own traumatic childhood then the sudden loss of her husband—my father—had thrust her into single parenthood without the tools to manage her grief while raising her children. In our community and era, taking care of your mental health wasn't celebrated as essential self-care—it came with judgment, fear, and unwanted labels that could follow you for life.

"She's not right in the head," they'd whisper about women who sought help. "She can't handle her business." In a world where Black women were expected to be unbreakable, admitting you were breaking carried shame too heavy to bear.

Understanding this doesn't excuse what happened—the wounds inflicted by a parent's words cut deeper than others. However, understanding has allowed me to practice the forgiveness that Christ modeled. "Father, forgive them, for they know not what they do," Jesus said from the cross. My mother didn't fully know what she was doing—how her words planted seeds that would take years to uproot.

As I raise my daughters now, I witness moments where her voice threatens to become mine. When frustration rises and harsh words form in my throat, I feel the generational pattern pulling at me like gravity. But this is where Christ's transformative power has been most evident in my life. "Therefore, if anyone is in Christ, the new creation has come: The old has gone, the new is here!" (2 Corinthians 5:17). Through His strength, not my own, I'm breaking cycles that have persisted for generations.

The seeds of criticism and shame planted in me will not find soil in my daughters. Instead, I'm intentionally planting seeds of affirmation, worth, and identity rooted in God's love. The generational curse ends with me—not because I'm stronger than those who came before, but because I've surrendered to a God specializing in redemption stories.

What Takes Root in Darkness

"For to me, to live is Christ and to die is gain."
(Philippians 1:21)

By freshman year of high school, the light and confidence that once radiated throughout had barely flickered. But there was more to my story than just lost confidence—there was also vulnerability that predators could sense.

What I could not articulate then was how the perfect storm had formed: a young girl desperate for validation, with fractured family support, and no understanding of her inherent worth in God's eyes. I became an easy target.

It started innocently enough—an older man offering attention, compliments, and a sense of maturity I craved. By fifteen, I was being trafficked, manipulated into a world I didn't understand through false promises and calculated grooming. The innocence that should have defined those years was stolen through a systematic process designed to break my will and separate me from anyone who might help.

After being coerced to meet up with promises of fun and Gifts, I found myself drugged and trapped in a basement bathroom. After being abused repeatedly. Sold to the highest bidder without my knowledge. Only realizing what was going on after trying to fight and scream, just to be told "shut the F- up! I already paid for you!"

The realization of my situation made my heart drop to the pit of my stomach, my mind raced with thoughts, and my mouth began to shut tight as I froze in fear. How long would I have to endure this? I cried, begging God to make it end. I ran to the door; it was locked. I screamed, and no one answered. I laid on the cold bathroom floor, the door cracking ever so slightly only to let the next man in. I searched the darkness for something to fight, even if it meant I would die. I welcomed death. A piece of me had already died as the rest of me grieved. " God, where are you? " I questioned for what felt like the thousandth time. The honk of a car horn released chaos into the house. Suddenly, I was being shoved out of the same bathroom I could not break free from.

Looking back, I can see how God's hand of protection remained even in those darkest moments—small interventions that prevented the worst possible outcomes, unexpected help that appeared at crucial moments, and an inner voice that kept a small flame of hope alive despite everything. Though I didn't recognize it as divine intervention then, the fact that I survived that period with my life intact was nothing short of God's grace manifesting in a situation where evil seemed to have complete control.

I remember the night I finally made it home after being missing. My mother's response was complex—a mixture of relief, anger, and helplessness that I could not understand then. "Where have you been? What's wrong with you?" she demanded, unable to see the manipulation and control that had ensnared me. In her eyes, I was making bad choices; she couldn't see I was a victim being systematically exploited.

"Nothing's wrong with me," I mumbled, she knew I was lying. To ashamed to admit what I just endured, a part of me wishing it was just a terrible dream. Unable to explain what was happening, afraid of not being believed, and already conditioned to protect my trafficker, I froze. My siblings snickered as my mom went in on me. I didn't think my day could get any worst yet somehow it had. With one slap to the face, I was silenced for 20 years. I sat there emotionless, holding in every tear until I couldn't any longer. When my mom finally allowed me to go to my room. I spent several hours trying to scrub away the pain and filth I felt, bathing with bleach hoping that it would somehow make me new. Or at least close enough to it. A pattern began, with my behavior growing more erratic and my mother's frustration deepening—neither of us equipped to name or address the actual problem.

As a mother raising daughters today in a world where this danger remains ever-present, I understand both perspectives. I navigate my own trauma and fear while trying to create a safe environment for my children that I lacked. Prayer has become my foundation, seeking the Lord's wisdom daily for discernment beyond my own limited vision.

There have been moments when divine intervention clearly protected my children—unexplained scheduling changes that kept them from dangerous situations, sudden insights that prompted me to check their communications at exactly the right moment, and community support appearing just when we needed them most. God's protective hand has been evident, turning my painful past into wisdom that helps shield my daughters.

For parents reading this, please know the signs of trafficking and exploitation:

- Sudden changes in behavior, friends, or clothing style
- Unexplained money, gifts, or possessions
- Increasing secrecy about whereabouts or communications
- Withdrawal from family and long-standing friends
- School problems, fatigue, or signs of physical abuse

- Older romantic partners or new friends with questionable influence
- Increasing isolation from normal support systems

Create an environment where your children know they can tell you anything without immediate judgment. Be vigilant about who can access your children, both online and in person. Talk openly about healthy relationships and boundaries from an early age. Most importantly, maintain a connection that makes them feel truly seen and valued—the void that predators most often exploit is the need to be valued.

Years passed, as I walked home from work one day, a chilling anticipation washed over me; soon, I would come face-to-face with my trafficker. The air grew tense as a delivery truck pulled behind me, its engine revving ominously. Suddenly, I hear someone inside frantically shouting my name, a voice I recognized all too well. I quicken my pace, determined to ignore the calls, but just a couple of blocks later, the truck swerves in front of me, cutting me off and forcing me to confront the dark shadows of my past. I froze in my steps, unable to move, a shiver running through me as I felt the cold metal pressing against my thigh. The weight of the box cutter I'd forgotten to put away before my lunch break filled me with an unexpected sense of boldness, a feeling I assumed was a sign from God.

With unwavering confidence, I stepped onto the delivery truck and asked, "What's up?" He asked if I wanted a ride, but I declined. Despite my refusal, he drove off anyway, expressing how much he had been thinking about me and how much he missed me.

As he drifted into memories of our last encounter, he wove
our shared moments into a whimsical fairytale, casting
aside the shadows of my nightmare and transforming his
grooming, manipulation, and trafficking into vibrant imag-
ery and enchanting possibilities.
As I reached into my pocket, I couldn't help but study his
movements, waiting for the perfect moment. He seemed so
comfortable and unsuspecting, as if he were encountering
the same 15-year-old he had known years ago. But I was
ready for what was about to unfold. This time, the tables
would turn, and he would experience the pain and hurt
he once inflicted on me. The anticipation built within me,
knowing the moment of vengeance drew near.
As he continued to speak, he began to tell me he had just
had a baby—a daughter. His face beamed with joy as he
pulled out pictures and talked about how smart she was.
I was conflicted. Wondering how someone so evil could
receive such a blessing? It's not fair! Just then, my heart began to soften as I imagined her growing up without a father,
feeling lost, abandoned, and unloved, just like me. I began
to feel an intense desire, one that I had not yet understood,
was the Holy Spirit. Tell me to pray for her, I didn't want
to, but the feeling wouldn't go away. So I prayed, in secret.
The father's sins would not meet the child, I prayed for her
protection, and though her father had done so much harm to
me, that she would see no harm. I prayed for this baby girl.
My trafficker's daughter, whom I had never met, I did not
know, but whose image remains ingrained in my mind to
this day.
A sharp "we're here! Snapped me out of my thoughts
immediately after whispering amen.
I was stunned, in complete amazement. I entered the truck
feeling tempted and desiring to do evil, and God used
that moment for good. I didn't care about being caught or
ruining my future or spending the rest of my life in jail. I

only wanted revenge but because I was obedient to the guidance of the Holy Spirit; God was able to save me and use me for good.

I didn't just come out unharmed, but the cement blocks, which were my burdens, once tied tightly around my ankles, causing me to want to drown, had been lifted. Not because I had a desire to forgive the person who abused me (or anyone else), but because God had a desire to set me free. A burden that I never expected to receive healing from, now suddenly gone.

Anger and a desire for revenge led me into that truck. Into a situation that could have risked my life and safety. Let me be clear: I do not recommend doing what I did. Never decide to confront your abuser alone; always call for emergency personnel and let them handle it. Always put your safety 1st.

For those who have experienced trafficking and/or abuse, know this: what happened to you was not your fault. The shame belongs to those who exploited you, not to you. I want to encourage you; it is time to unload the baggage that our pain and trauma have left us with. When we refuse to submit our burdens to the Lord, we unintentionally submit them to our children and those closest to us. And despite our best efforts, we continue the cycle of generational curses, we did not even realize existed. A harsh reality I've only learned after years of trying and failing. It's time to break chains and generational cycles. It's time to declare freedom over your bloodline.

Healing is possible. God sees you, knows every moment of your pain, and offers restoration that can transform even the deepest wounds into testimony.

"He heals the brokenhearted and binds up their wounds."
(Psalm 147:3)

If you know or suspect that you or someone you know is being sex trafficked, contact the National Human Trafficking Hotline at 1-888-373-7888. They can connect you with local resources and help create a safety plan.

Chapter 4

The Veil Lifts

When Death Came Calling

"For to me, to live is Christ and to die is gain." (Philippians 1:21)

I woke up from what I thought was my sleep, though later, I would question whether I had truly awakened or entered a different kind of consciousness altogether. My body felt wrong—heavy yet disconnected. My throat burned with a soreness, unlike any illness I'd experienced, as though something foreign was lodged there, preventing me from swallowing or speaking. My head felt weighted like someone had filled it with sand, yet strangely, I felt no pain.

The first sound that registered was soft weeping— unfamiliar yet somehow recognizable. I saw my mother crying quietly in a corner. My mother the woman who had weathered loss, homelessness, and single parenthood without shedding a tear—was now sobbing softly, her shoulders trembling with grief. Something profound was happening, something that had finally broken her unbreakable spirit. In that moment of confusion, I didn't realize, that something, was me...

I noticed a large man consoling her, hugging her so tightly that I couldn't see his face. I tried to get their attention, but she just continued crying. I attempted to speak, but no words came out. I cleared my throat and tried to yell as loudly as I could.

"Mom! What's wrong?" she just cried, her head hanging low. "Mom... mom!" I screamed, but she didn't even budge. I thought to myself that something must be terribly wrong. I had never seen my mom cry. Through all the things she had endured, I'd watched her struggle, fight, and ultimately prevail, yet I had never seen her shed tears. Panic began to rise within me. I wanted her to know that I was okay, I decided to get up and get her attention, since she couldn't hear me. I turned to the side of the bed and summoned all my strength to lift myself up. I walked over to my mom, trying to capture her attention.

"We are surrounded by so great a cloud of witnesses..." (Hebrews 12:1)

But the man stood in the way. He wore a black tuxedo, as if he'd just stepped off a wedding cake, and his hair was styled in a jerry curl, reminiscent of the 80s.

The man's profile seemed strangely familiar, triggering fragments of memories I couldn't quite piece together. Who was this man comforting my mother? Why would she bring a stranger during what was a profoundly personal crisis? My confusion quickly shifted to irritation—how long had he been in her life while I was unconscious?

Then he shifted slightly, and I caught a glimpse of his face.

The recognition hit me with the force of revelation. It couldn't be—and yet it was. DAD!!" I screamed through tears that seemed to come from somewhere deeper than my eyes. My father, who had died when I was just two years old, whose absence had shaped our entire family dynamic, whose name 'Lil Mac Chewy' had once brought me childish pride, was standing in this hospital room.

The impossible nature of this realization didn't strike me immediately. Instead, I felt a desperate need for acknowledgement. "Can you see me?" I pleaded, waving my arms, trying to intercept his gaze. But his eyes remained fixed on my mother, his attention entirely devoted to comforting her grief. Even in this supernatural moment, I remained invisible, caught between worlds— seen by neither the living nor the dead.

A thought penetrated my confusion: if my father, who had died decades ago, was visibly present, what did that mean about my state of being? The boundary between life and death suddenly seemed thinner than I had imagined.

I backed away from my father and mother, overwhelmed by questions without answers. Disoriented, I retreated toward the hospital bed—the one place that promised clarity or at least rest from this confusion.

As I approached, I noticed someone was already lying there. The realization came in increasing intensity: first curiosity, then confusion, horror as recognition dawned. I was looking down at myself—my physical body, still and silent amid tubes and monitors. My head was shaved, gauze wrapped around it with blood-stained bandages visible beneath. A medical device protruded from my skull. My neck had been surgically opened, held apart by a medical instrument. Various tubes ran down my nose while IVs fed into my arms. Despite this trauma, my face had an expression of unnatural peace, like an empty vessel awaiting its inhabitant's return.

"Oh, Shabriya," I whispered, "what happened to you?"

In that moment, Scripture I hadn't thought about in years suddenly illuminated this experience: "For we know that if our earthly house, this tent, is destroyed, we have a building from God, a house not made with hands, eternal in the heavens" (2 Corinthians 5:1). Was I experiencing what Paul had described—the separation of spirit from bodily "tent"? My Catholic school teaching about body and soul being distinct yet unified suddenly made sense in a way no theology class had ever conveyed.

There was something profoundly humbling about seeing my physical body separate from my consciousness, realizing that what I had always identified as "me" was a complex partnership between flesh and spirit. In that hospital room, I began to understand that my identity transcended my physical form in ways I had never contemplated.

The last thing I could remember was being on a gurney, rushed into emergency surgery. They wouldn't explain everything that was happening, but I knew it was serious. I had passed out and lost my strength after feeling a pop in my brain. I felt myself being hurried away, though I couldn't see anything. As I sat waiting for access outside the doors of the operating unit, I heard a familiar voice calling my name. "Shabriya! SHABRIYA!" Is that Shayla? I thought. I tried to get up, but I could not lift my weight. "Can you hear me?!" she yelled. I tried to speak, but I couldn't even open my mouth. I thought and told my body what to do, but my brain wasn't connecting. I tried to open my eyes; they barely creaked open, only to catch a glimpse of her sliding down the wall, crying, as the doors began to open. Just before they rolled me out, she got up and yelled, "If you can hear me, move your hand, please, if you can hear me!"

I tried, I tried so hard, but I couldn't lift my arm. I focused on my fingers and began to pray. It felt as if time had paused. God, I'm praying; please allow me to move my arm if You can. God, please, I need them to have hope I will make it. I need them to have faith, Lord, please. I kept trying; it took all my strength and effort, but something finally moved—just a few fingers. A burst of energy surged through my arm, giving me enough strength to move ever so slightly right before being wheeled away. Shayla screamed in excitement. "See, she CAN hear me!" I was happy she saw it. I was glad she could tell the family. Then the nurse responded, "That's just a twitch; sometimes the body just does that." I listened to that nurse shatter my sister's faith, shatter the faith I needed them to have, all because she did not believe. "Oh", Shayla whispered, sounding defeated, as the doors closed behind us.

Damn! I thought as I drifted off to sleep.

Staring at my broken body, anger and despair welled up from somewhere deep within me. Not the shallow anger of inconvenience but the profound rage from facing mortality without preparation.

"Lord, why me?" I cried out into the emptiness of the hospital room. "Why this? Why now?" My silent cries carried all the anguish of a life that felt incomplete, unfair, and cut short.

"Why not?" came a response that wasn't audible yet penetrated more deeply than sound ever could.

I paused, startled. The voice wasn't external or even internal in the way my thoughts were. It simply existed as though the truth had always been there, waiting to be noticed. I couldn't say with certainty it was God speaking, yet something in me recognized an authority beyond human wisdom in those two simple words.

"I don't deserve this," I protested, summoning the indignation of someone who believes suffering should be proportional to sin.

"Who does?" the voice replied, not unkindly but firmly.

The question wasn't rhetorical—it invited genuine reflection. What made me believe anyone "deserved" suffering more than me? What calculations had I made to determine that others should bear the pain while I remained exempt? People everywhere were suffering—children with illnesses, mothers losing babies, families torn apart by violence—and here I was, asking for special consideration.

The exchange stripped away layers of entitlement I hadn't recognized in myself. God wasn't saying my suffering was deserved or good—only that suffering doesn't operate on a system of cosmic fairness that humans can comprehend. As Scripture says, the rain falls on the just and unjust alike, as does hardship.

"Ugh", my head felt like it had exploded. Something may have occurred in the operating room. But why would I be here? Looking at myself, I was confused; I thought to myself, this must be a dream. It has to be. I examined my body again before returning to bed and going to sleep. I tried to awaken my body but couldn't; I didn't attempt to get up again. For days, I lay there, afraid that the next time, I might not be able to return to my body. I merely slept for what seemed like months. I was trapped in a dream cycle unlike any dream I've ever had. Everything was so real; it felt as if I was watching my life play out in a different reality, a different realm. I was still Shabriya; I just made different choices and had different outcomes. I could hear a man praying over me and reading the Bible constantly. It was as if it were playing in my mind like it was on speaker. (Like when you're shopping in a department store).

Between Worlds and Revelations

"Do not forget to show hospitality to strangers, for by
so doing some people have shown hospitality to angels
without knowing it." (Hebrews 13:2)

Time lost meaning in that strange space between worlds.
I drifted in and out of awareness, though whether days
passed, I couldn't say. One day I sensed a new presence in
my hospital room.

Opening my spiritual eyes, I saw that a man had come to
visit me. Unlike the medical staff who moved through my
room, checking vitals and adjusting equipment, this visitor
seemed aware of my body in the bed and my conscious
presence, observing from beside it. He had beautiful, rich,
dark skin that seemed to radiate its light, and his locks
were long, full, and healthy, cascading past his shoulders.
Though I couldn't see his face—it remained beyond full
recognition, like trying to look directly at the sun—his presence brought an immediate sense of peace that transcended
understanding.

There was something ancient yet timeless about him. He
carried no clipboard and wore no white coat or scrubs, yet
he moved with the confidence of someone who belonged
there more rightfully than anyone else. His presence felt
simultaneously foreign and deeply familiar, like remember-
ing something I had always known but somehow forgotten.

Most striking was the complete absence of fear I felt in his
company. In a situation that should have terrified me—

being separated from my body, hovering between life and death—his presence brought a safety I hadn't experienced since childhood, perhaps not even then. It wasn't merely the absence of danger but the presence of complete acceptance and love.

"You're not alone," he communicated, though no audible words passed between us. Somehow, I understood him perfectly, more clearly than spoken language would have allowed.

Was this an angel? A manifestation of divine presence? Or was it something my traumatized brain had created for comfort? I had no theological framework to process this encounter fully, yet something in my spirit recognized him as a messenger from beyond the physical realm.

I couldn't talk, but he still understood me. He was so compassionate and caring. He even came every day to be with me and help me recover. He taught me sign language because I was worried, I would not be able to communicate when I woke up. He always assured me that everything would be all right and that even if life were different, I should have faith in God that everything would work out for my good.

While I was in the hospital, I dreamed of being outside; I craved fresh air. (I still detest the stale smell of hospitals.) After spending so much time indoors, I yearned for the warm sun and cool breeze. I knew that every time he came to the hospital, he was coming to take me outside. He would walk me through the most beautiful gardens, full of butterflies, lush green grass, and tall trees. The sun always shone there, and the birds sang lovely melodies. He pushed me in my wheelchair along the way, but when I was with him, I didn't need it. When we were together, it felt like nothing had ever happened. I wasn't paralyzed; I was never hurt; I was never taken advantage of; I never bore the weight of helping my mom raise her children; I never experienced loss, and I never endured this traumatic event. Only love and happiness. Just him and me; I felt like our souls intertwined. He knew me and loved me through all my pain. I was so at peace. I had never felt peace like this; I had never felt this free and open. It was an unexplainable feeling of serenity and love that I never wanted to leave. He wanted to show me a better life, and I loved and accepted him for it.

The Stroke That Revealed Eternity

"The thief comes only to steal and kill and destroy; I have come that they may have life, and have it to the full." (John 10:10)

My encounters with the mysterious visitor continued, increasing peace and even moments of joy amid my dire circumstances. But as with any light, the darkness seemed determined to extinguish it.

Later one night, after the visitor departed, my room's atmosphere changed dramatically. The peaceful sanctuary it had become in his presence transformed into something sinister. The soft glow of night lights took on an ominous quality, casting shadows that seemed to move with intentionality. The hospital corridor outside my room, once merely institutional, now felt haunted, as though lost souls wandered there, trapped between worlds as I was.

The night nurse who entered my room no longer appeared as a caregiver but as a threat. When she poured water to clear my breathing tube—a routine medical procedure—my spiritual perception interpreted it as an attempt to drown me. Terror gripped me as I fought against restraints I hadn't noticed before, pulling at tubes that kept my physical body alive while my spiritual self, panicked.

What I was experiencing felt like war—not between doctors and illness, but between light and darkness, hope and despair, life and death. Though I lacked the theological language to describe it then, I was witnessing firsthand what Scripture calls "our struggle not against flesh and blood, but against the rulers, against the authorities, against the powers of this dark world and against the spiritual forces of evil in the heavenly realms" (Ephesians 6:12).

These terrifying episodes always came after moments of spiritual clarity and peace, as though my growing awareness and connection to the divine visitor threatened something. The pattern itself seemed significant: revelation followed by attack, insight followed by confusion, peace followed by terror. It mirrored the spiritual journey I would later understand more fully—how moments of greatest spiritual breakthrough often precede the fiercest opposition.

I was afraid, I begged God to take me out of that nightmare. Soon after, I woke up. I noticed my daughter's father, Ben, putting flowers in a vase in the room. "Hey, sleepy head," he said sweetly. I'm so happy you're finally up.

I was confused about why he was here. The last time we spoke, I begged him to pick up our 2-year-old daughter while I was in the E.R., scared and fighting for my life. He refused. He did not care about my situation or what would happen to our daughter if no one showed up to get her. He told me how much he hated me before; he made it his mission to make my life miserable. Yet here he was, acting like nothing ever happened.

I tried to speak but couldn't form words. Where is he? I thought desperately. Where is the man who had shown me such kindness in that spiritual realm? My confused mind, still struggling to differentiate between spiritual experience and earthly desires, had begun to transform this mysterious visitor into something more familiar - a protector, a savior, a spouse.

This wasn't a divine revelation but my own vulnerability speaking - my flesh and wounded spirit desperately seeking comfort in familiar human terms. In my disoriented state, I had taken the spiritual kindness I had experienced and reframed it through my earthly longing for protection and care. "Surely, he has to save me from this!" I thought, my mind clinging to the idea that anyone would rescue me from this bewildering reality.

The mysterious visitor whose presence had comforted me in that in-between state had become, in my confused thinking, the husband-protector I had always yearned for. It wasn't about romantic love but security - my mind's way of processing spiritual comfort through the lens of my most fundamental human needs. I felt utterly abandoned, thrust back into harsh reality without this presence.

Ben kept talking. He went on and on about how worried they were. I looked him over and noticed his clothes and shoes were nice and looked expensive. What is he up to? I thought. In the six years I had known him, he had never worked. He refused to help with our daughter, unless it benefited him. He tried to convince me that he had changed and almost losing me made him realize he wanted us to be a family.

Unable to respond, I stopped looking at him and stared at the floor. All I wanted was my husband and the peace he once provided. I continued feeling him, but not as strongly as before.

Ben stepped out to let my nurses know I had finally woken up. They all flooded in, including my mom, with Kam. I was so happy to see her, but she had gotten so big. How long have I been asleep? I thought to myself. I had missed so much, I started to cry, tears falling down my face. Ben reached over and hugged me. I missed you. I love you so much, he whispered. I was pissed at this show he was putting on. I was pissed I couldn't call him out on his lies, and I was livid he was touching me. Where is my husband? I yelled, but no words came out. I tried to yell for Ben not to touch me again, but nothing. I was terrified, but I was still restrained. I tried to push away but I was quickly reminded of my limitations, that I was paralyzed. No matter how hard I tried to tell my brain what to do, my body would not respond. It was as if my brain was misfiring all day and could not connect to the other parts of my body.

> **"For our struggle is not against flesh and blood, but against...the spiritual forces of evil in the heavenly realms."** (Ephesians 6:12)

Each day, I grew more frantic and more annoyed. I wondered how long Ben could possibly keep this up. What is he going to do once I recover? Maybe he thinks I'm not going to recover. Why else would he do this? I thought.

"Hello," he answered hushedly, moving away from my bed. I couldn't distinguish the words from the caller, but the feminine voice was unmistakable.

"I know, I know. They all believe me. Everything's going as planned," he whispered.

"She hasn't woken up in days, and I'm sure she'll be gone soon. I'll be rich. You know what I mean. What's mine is yours, right? Yes, babe, you can have whatever you want."

Though physically incapacitated, my spiritual discernment had never been sharper. Scripture says, "For our struggle is not against flesh and blood, but against...the spiritual forces of evil in the heavenly realms" (Ephesians 6:12). At that moment, I recognized Ben's deception as more than human opportunism—it was spiritual warfare targeting me when I was most vulnerable.

The enemy often attacks when we're at our weakest, using those closest to us as instruments. Ben couldn't know that my time between worlds had given me supernatural clarity to see through pretense. The same God who had shown me spiritual reality during my coma was now revealing the truth behind Ben's performance of devotion.

I thought to myself, "Wow, my life really turned into a telenovela, and what money? Social security? Money for Kam? (I mean, we did have shared custody of our daughter, but I wasn't dead yet!) Insurance? "Wow, what a bum, this is ridiculous. "At that moment, I decided that if this was going to be my life, I might as well just stay asleep.

"For my thoughts are not your thoughts, neither are your ways my ways," declares the LORD." (Isaiah 55:8)

I retreated from consciousness, slipping back into the depths of a coma for what felt like years. The betrayal had broken something in me—my will to fight, perhaps even my will to live. From that darkness, I cried out: "Lord, I'm tired.?"

I realized it was my time to go.

God! I yelled.... God! HEY... I know you're here. I felt his holiness but could not see him, and he said nothing. Lord, I thank you for everything you have blessed me with. I repent for my sins, big and small, known and unknown. I started a list of things I've done. I'm sorry for having sex before marriage. I'm sorry for not worshiping you. I'm sorry for being a liar. I'm sorry for doubting you. I'm sorry for turning my back on you. Thank you for never abandoning me. And I'm ready to join you in heaven... It was silent. I yelled, "It's okay. Seriously, I want to be with you." (As if he needed my permission.) OK, I'm tired of being alone. I want to reunite with my family.

Immediately, I found myself back in my hospital room—not in my physical body but observing from above as medical staff rushed around the bed where my earthly form lay. A light unlike anything in this world shone from above, radiating not just brightness but perfect peace, complete acceptance, and overwhelming love. I recognized it instinctively as the threshold between earthly existence and eternity—the passage Scripture hints at when it speaks of "the valley of the shadow of death" (Psalm 23:4).

As I gazed toward this radiance, I saw figures emerging at its edges—my grandmother and great-grandmother, Mother, whose spiritual guidance had shaped my childhood faith. They appeared not as the elderly women they had been at death but restored to the fullness of who they were, perfected and whole. Standing slightly behind them were others I somehow recognized, though we had never met in life—generations of family who had gone before.

At that moment, I understood what Scripture means about being "surrounded by so great a cloud of witnesses" (Hebrews 12:1). These weren't just memories or imaginings but spiritual presences at this threshold between worlds. Their eyes held wisdom beyond anything earthly, yet they remained distinctly themselves. They weren't there to welcome me or guide me across—their presence seemed more like witnesses to this moment of decision, neither pulling me toward them nor pushing me back toward life. They simply existed in that space of in-between, as though observing rather than participating in what would come next.

I watched as the Doctor rushed in. I watched my mom being pushed out. I watched as my dad was still with her.

> *"He will turn the hearts of the parents to their children, and the hearts of the children to their parents."* (Malachi 4:6)

As I began to walk toward the light, determined to leave earthly struggles behind, a figure stepped directly into my path—my father. Not the distant memory constructed from others' stories, not the man from old photographs, but fully present and real. His expression was stern yet filled with love, his eyes locked with mine for the first time since I was two years old.

"Shabriya," he said, my name in his voice triggering emotions I never knew I carried. Do you not see what you're doing?!"

His words carried an authority that stopped me instantly. This was the voice I had longed to hear my entire life—the father whose absence had shaped everything.

"Look at your mom!" he continued, gesturing toward where she stood weeping beside my hospital bed. "Do you know how much this will hurt her? Do you know how much this will hurt them? Their lives won't be better if you choose not to fight." His voice softened slightly. "She's still hurting from losing me after all these years. How do you think this will make things better?"

At that moment, I understood something profound about God's design for families—how the absence of my earthly father had created a wound that had affected every relationship since. Yet here, at this threshold between worlds, God had granted us this moment of connection, this opportunity for my father to fulfill, if only briefly, the protective role he'd been unable to provide in life.

"I don't think caring for me would be a better option," I protested, though my resolve weakened. "I want to be with you guys. I'm tired of fighting. I'm tired of being alone."

"GO BACK!" he commanded with parental authority I had never experienced but instantly recognized. "My child is not a quitter."

My child. Two words I had waited a lifetime to hear. In them was an acknowledgment, claiming, and identity— everything I had sought in relationships and achievements. I studied his face, memorizing every detail, knowing instinctively this might be our only conversation until eternity.

I studied his face for a minute. This was the first time I'd seen or talked to my dad in 22 years, and here I was, trying to convince him that everything would be better if I, too, were dead. I could be with you...

It's not your time, he whispered. I could see the hurt and fear on his face. I love you; I said as I turned around and headed back. They were right; I was more concerned about potentially being a burden. I had lost sight of faith and hope, I had stopped fighting, and I convinced myself that my death was the best option. I went back to sit in my earth-bound body for the last time.

"God, I yelled. God help!!! Well, I know you're here somewhere... I called on God once again. This time, I begged Him for a second chance at life. "Please, Lord!" I cried out, my soul trembling with urgency. "I'm ready now—ready to fight for my life! I've been so wrong, preparing for death when I should have been clinging to the life You gave me. I surrender everything to Your will! Not my plan, timeline, or understanding—only Yours. I believe with every fiber of my being that whatever path You've marked for me is the right one, even if I can't see where it leads. I'll follow it blindly, trustingly."

My pleas echoed in the silence. Had I realized too late? Would he still hear me after I'd spent so long turning away?

"I've been so foolish, trying to control everything instead of seeking Your guidance. Forgive me for thinking I knew better than You, for doubting Your presence when You never once left my side. It was you all along—in the darkness, silence, and waiting. You were there, and I was too stubborn to see it."

The desperation in my spirit grew as I received no answer. Had I squandered my chance?

"Thank you for saving me when I didn't deserve saving. Thank you for every blessing I've taken for granted. God, I trust Your will completely now—whatever it means, whatever it costs. Your desires are my desires now. Nothing else matters. I'm sorry, Lord. I'm so sorry."

I prayed all day. Although I thought I had messed up, I believed that God would hear my" prayers.

> **"Draw near to God, and he will draw near to you."** (James 4:8)

The next morning, I began to pray with a desperation and sincerity I had never known. "Please Lord, please forgive me for my sins. Help Lord! Please, Lord help!"

In that moment, reality itself seemed to shift. The atmosphere around me transformed—not visibly, but perceptibly to some deeper sense beyond the physical. I felt a presence enter that space, vast beyond comprehension, intimate beyond explanation. The presence was heavy—not with weight or burden, but with the incomprehensible fullness of perfect holiness, absolute power, and complete knowledge. It filled every molecule of air, every atom of my being.

This encounter was unlike any visitation before; even standing face-to-face with my deceased father had not awakened the depth of what I felt in this moment.

This was utterly different—the Creator among His creation. I knew without doubt that God Himself had drawn near, that the veil between His realm and mine had become momentarily transparent. Scripture says, "The heavens, even the highest heaven, cannot contain you" (1 Kings 8:27), yet somehow His presence concentrated in that hospital room, focused on me in my brokenness.

I felt simultaneously utterly unworthy and completely loved—like Isaiah crying, "Woe is me!" while being cleansed by divine fire. Terror and joy mingled indistinguishably. Peace washed through me—not the absence of trouble but the presence of something so complete it made earthly concerns seem distant and small. It was a peace that "transcends all understanding" (Philippians 4:7), incomparable to anything in earthly experience.

Most astonishing was His posture toward me. The God who spoke galaxies into existence, who commanded angels and held existence itself in being, did not speak command or instruct. He listened. The Creator attended to me, His creation, with perfect focus and infinite patience. In that holy silence lay more communication than all human words combined could convey.

Lord, I begged. I'm sorry, I'm sorry for everything. You are all-knowing, all-powerful. Please, Lord if it is your will... Please, Lord, I need to wake up.

Awake

My eyes shot open with an intensity that startled even me. I looked around, disoriented yet certain—I was back in my body. My spirit, which had traveled through realms beyond physical understanding, was now tethered again to flesh and bone, to pain and limitation.

'Finally! I'm up,' I thought, attempting to speak these words aloud, but only managed a weak movement of my lips. My throat felt like sandpaper, raw and constricted from the breathing tube. My head throbbed with each heartbeat, a relentless reminder that I had returned to a damaged vessel.

The peaceful weightlessness I had experienced in that spiritual realm was gone, replaced by the heaviness of a body that barely responded to my commands. This wasn't just waking up from sleep or even from a medical procedure—this was a soul returning to its earthly dwelling after glimpsing eternity. The contrast was jarring, almost cruel. Yet beneath the physical discomfort flickered a profound certainty: I had been sent back for a purpose. The same God who had revealed Himself to me in those between-worlds moments had determined that my time on earth was not finished.

"For you have delivered my soul from death, my eyes from tears, and my feet from falling." (Psalm 116:8)

I had promised to return for my daughter, and God had honored that commitment. Now, I would need to honor mine.

I tried to sit up in my bed, but I looked down, and my hands were restrained. I tried to slip them out. I saw someone approaching the door. You're up, the doctor and nurse entered the room, startled to see me awake. I immediately tried to yell for my mom, but I could only mouth the words. MY MOM, MOM, I mouthed to the nurse, hoping she could read my lips. Your mom stepped out, but she will be so happy you're awake.

"Shabriya, do you know where you are?" the doctor asked, his voice gentle but clinical.

I managed a weak "Yes."

"Where are you?"

"Hospital," I whispered, each syllable requiring tremendous effort.

"Yes, you're at... " He slowly spoke the Hospital's name, as if he were waiting for me to remember. "Do you remember what happened to you?"

I shook my head no, the simple movement sending sharp pains through my skull.

"You had a brain bleed. You were rushed into emergency surgery."

His words floated in the space between us. *A brain bleed?* My thoughts were thick, sluggish.

"Do you know what today is?"

Before I could respond, darkness pulled me back under. The combination of medication, trauma, and exhaustion overwhelmed my consciousness. It felt as if someone was repeatedly striking my head.

My mother's anxious face hovered over me when I opened my eyes. I tried to say "Mom," but my lips moved silently, no sound emerging. The drugs coursing through my system made focusing nearly impossible.

The transformation in her expression when she realized I was awake was unlike anything I'd ever witnessed. Pure joy replaced fear; her face illuminated from within.

"Yes! We did it!" she exclaimed, impulsively hugging the startled nurse.

"Shabriya?" she asked, her voice trembling with hope.

I managed a slow nod; the smallest movement I could offer as confirmation I was still here.

This display of raw emotion stunned me. Throughout my childhood, my mother had rarely shown vulnerability—not sadness, tears, hurt, or even joy. She existed primarily in states of anger or detachment. I'd seen glimpses of happiness occasionally, but they were rare, fleeting moments in an otherwise stoic existence. Life had dealt her difficult cards too, yet she had always supported us through everything—good, bad, or indifferent. Her presence was the one constant I could depend on.

Seeing her face transformed by relief and joy, I realized how close I must have come to death. She looked as though she'd witnessed the impossible—as if she'd seen me return from beyond. I recognized the truth in her eyes: she had just witnessed a miracle.

I struggled to communicate how happy I was to see her, but my efforts produced only silence.

"It's alright, just rest," the nurse said softly, adjusting my IV.

For the first time in what felt like forever, I surrendered to sleep, knowing it was finally safe to let go.

The next few days unfolded in a blur of medical assess-
ments. My days began with the early hospital rhythm,
the 6 a.m. rounds marking the start of another day in this
sterile world.

The neurosurgeon appeared one morning, his face wearing
the practiced cheerfulness of someone who delivers both
miracles and devastation daily. "Ms. Hill, I'm glad to see
you awake," he said, his voice carrying a brightness that
felt out of place amid the beeping monitors and antiseptic
smell. "Your surgery went well, though you scared us!"

I watched nervously as he examined me, his hands moving with practiced efficiency while he spoke in medical
shorthand to the nurses—words and phrases that floated
above my understanding. My entire world had narrowed to
this bed, these walls, and the mysterious workings of my
broken body.

He moved with confident quickness from one side of my
hospital bed to the other, his pen poised for the sensory test
I didn't yet understand would change everything. The cool
metal tip touched my right arm. "Can you feel this?"

I nodded yes, relief momentarily washing through me.
"Good, good." The same test on my left arm and hand
yielded the same positive results, and I allowed myself a
small measure of hope.

"Wonderful," he said, his tone subtly shifting as he moved
toward the foot of the bed.

"Can you feel this?"

I looked down, my perspective from the hospital bed
allowing me to see his pen tracing patterns along my left

foot. I could see the pressure he applied and the movement, but sensation had vanished, as though that part of my body belonged to someone else. I felt nothing. Absolutely nothing.

I squeezed my eyes shut, fighting to control the tears threatening to spill. The crushing weight of understanding descended: this wasn't temporary weakness. Something fundamental had been severed.

Slowly, I shook my head. "No."

The surgeon's face revealed nothing, but his voice softened slightly. "I see." He continued the assessment, moving to my leg with a small tool. "Tell me if you feel this. I'm going to prick you a little, but don't worry, it won't hurt."

The irony of his words hung in the air between us. It wouldn't hurt because I couldn't feel it at all. I watched as he tested my leg with the small instrument, the skin dimpling under the pressure. Still nothing. He moved to my right foot, and again, there was only the visual confirmation that he was touching me—no sensation whatsoever.

With each negative response, the reality crystallized: I was paralyzed. The words hadn't been spoken aloud yet, but the truth was clearly written across my consciousness. The body I had taken for granted, the simple act of feeling my legs and feet—gone, perhaps forever.

I watched as all the nurses and doctors scribbled notes, their concerned expressions telling me more than their clinical words. The atmosphere in the room grew heavier with each shake of my head.

'Miss Hill, can you feel this?' the doctor asked, moving to my right leg.

I gave a deep sigh and slowly shook my head. 'No.'

"My flesh and my heart may fail, but God is the strength of my heart and my portion forever." (Psalm 73:26)

The finality of that simple word hung in the air. 'Wow, so I'm going to be paralyzed. I won't be able to walk,' I thought, the reality sinking like a stone dropping through water. I moved freely through beautiful gardens just days ago with my spiritual companion. Now I couldn't feel the prick of a pin on my own flesh.

At that moment, something unexpected happened within me. Instead of panic or despair, I felt a strange sense of acceptance. 'Can I be mad?' I questioned myself. 'I asked God that His will be done in my life. I guess this is God's will, right?'

The prayer I had offered in that spiritual realm— surrendering completely to God's purpose—now faced its first earthly test. Would I still trust Him when His will meant limitation? When it would mean dependence? When it would mean a life that was nothing like what I had planned?

I was disappointed but didn't want the Lord to think I was ungrateful. I understood with a clarity that surprised me that it was by His will alone that I was alive and awakened. The miracle wasn't that I should walk again—the miracle was that I had been given another chance at life in any form.

I quickly moved past my disappointment and refocused on the doctor. I refused to sit sad and disappointed after receiving such a beautiful gift, this miracle of continued existence from the Lord. If paralysis were part of my testimony, then I would embrace it as the path God had chosen for me.

The doctor tested the rest of my lower body with the same pricking motion. I shook my head "no" while trying to keep my disappointment from showing. A sudden wave of fear and worry overwhelmed me, bringing doubts I couldn't control. Thoughts crashed through my mind: How would I care for my daughter? How would I take care of myself? My entire life would be completely different—I couldn't handle this.

"Okay, squeeze my finger," the doctor directed, interrupting my spiral. "Miss Hill!" he prompted when I didn't immediately respond.

I concentrated on squeezing as hard as possible, knowing my grip was weak. The doctor continued his assessment methodically.

"Okay, now push... pull. Good job. Now, this hand. Squeeze as tight as you can."

"Good job," he affirmed. "No worries, Ms. Hill. We'll have you start working with the physical therapist. Can you say hello?"

I opened my mouth and attempted to speak as loudly as possible but produced no sound.

Oh Lord, how am I going to get through this? I thought.

"Let's get the speech therapist in here today," he instruct-
ed, replacing my oxygen mask. "Okay, Ms. Hill, you look
good. We're going to focus on controlling the pain. You'll
start physical therapy, speech therapy, and occupational
therapy soon. You'll have a nurse perform some lung exercises with you. We are going to take excellent care of you."

His chipper voice, calm demeanor and promise of "good
care" didn't do much to ease my worries. I was overwhelmed at the thought of being paralyzed and how
difficult that would make life for me and my daughter.
Thoughts of being to "broken" to care for her flooded my
mind, I quickly ignored them. An unsuccessful attempt to
accept my fate. These thoughts of being too broken would
become a reoccurring theme along my journey, fueling my
doubt and confusion.

During that first 1-2 weeks after waking up from my coma,
I had a very difficult time understanding what was real. As
I spent all this time, what I thought was years, being alone
and navigating this spiritual realm, where I was perfectly
fine and healthy. My 2 realities ran side by side. I often had
trouble discerning my earthly life from this spiritual one.

These moments of confusion and blurred realities would
later plant seeds of distrust during seasons of revelation.

The stark contrast between good and evil, light and darkness, subtle lies that grew into chaotic moments—all
created a fog I couldn't navigate alone. Leaving me seemingly "paranoid" during moments of warfare. Seeking
to be hidden from the same judgment and "crazy" title I
watched my mother navigate alone, as a child. In times of
mental distress, "Is this real? Is this God? Is this a trap or

scheme of the enemy?" would become a consistent line of questioning, as I desperately prayed for clarity yet finding none. Until I opened His Word and began to study His voice.

"My sheep hear my voice, and I know them, and they follow me." (John 10:27)

As the new week began, my day was packed with therapy. The first day of my physical therapy, I was excited. I was determined to walk again, and I believed this would help. The therapist began to ask me questions to help me understand my memory loss.

Do you know where we are? I wrote yes. Do you know who our president is? I shook my head and thought, "How do I know when I've been sleeping for 10 years?" Do you know what happened that brought you in? No, I pointed it out. Do you know what year it is? I used my fingers to give her the date 2… 0… 2… 3. She asked again. Do you know what year it is? I was very irritated because I just told her. This time she had me write it down 2…. 0… 2... 3… I wrote sloppily

Do you think that it is 2023? I shook my head, yes, obviously. Miss Hill, it is 2013, you've only been asleep for three weeks. Obama is still our president. And you are here because you had a brain bleed. In my coma state in between realms, time moved differently. I had done so much, lived so many lives in those 3 weeks, I was a completely different person. My mind just could not grasp how little time had actually gone by.

We moved on to exercises and therapy.

We started by pulling myself up into the sitting position. She taught me ways to support myself and pull myself up without the help of my legs. At that time, Ben busted in, flowers in hand. My love, we are so happy that you're awake.

I stared at him, confusion and growing dread mingling in my chest. I looked him up and down—button-up shirt, polished dress shoes, fresh haircut—so different from his usual careless appearance. Something felt terribly wrong, like I was experiencing déjà vu from a nightmare I couldn't quite remember. My eyes widened as he confidently greeted the doctor and smoothly introduced himself as 'my other half'—a claim so false it made my skin crawl.

"No weapon formed against you shall prosper, and every tongue which rises against you in judgment, You shall condemn." (Isaiah 54:17)

He asked for a vase for his flowers and if he could sit in on my physical therapy, performing the role of devoted partner with such conviction that even I almost believed it for a moment. I was terrified as he pulled the seat beside me, ignoring my head shaking 'no' with increasing desperation.

At that moment, I understood what Scripture meant about spiritual warfare in a way I hadn't ever understood before. Here was evil masquerading as care, predation disguised as protection. This was what it meant to be 'delivered into the hands of men'—vulnerable, voiceless, unable to defend myself against someone determined to exploit my weakness.

The presence I had felt in the spiritual realm—that divine protector who had walked with me through gardens and distant shores—seemed impossibly far away now. Where was that comfort, that security? Why would God allow me to be so exposed to someone who meant me harm? Like a sheep among wolves, I felt abandoned, with no shepherd in sight.

Yet something within me—some steel that hadn't been there before my near-death experience—refused to give in to despair. If God had brought me back to life, surely, He hadn't brought me back to be victimized. If He had given me a second chance, surely, He would also provide a way through this valley. I might lack physical strength and even the ability to speak, but I still had the will to fight.

He started to grab my hand and massage it. I instantly got away. "Oh, honey, it's OK, it's just me." I started to hit him as hard as I could, barely touching him but hoping to raise awareness towards my growing discomfort. unable to talk, I grunted and pushed him away in an effort to alert the therapist that I did not feel comfortable. He gently took my hand and rubbed it, left a long kiss on my head and face, and then looked my therapist in the eye as he lied, "Oh, she's just playing," he laughed. "These are just love taps," he looked at me and smiled ear to ear

Aww, OK, she responded. Gushing as if she had just seen a cute puppy. As I sat in fear, I thought, is she serious? I started to point at him and point to the door, fighting, exhausting every ounce of strength I owned, to just barely push him off me as he tried to caress and massage me... What the hell is wrong with him? I thought as panic took over. In a last-ditch effort, I looked my therapist dead in her soul and pointed at him and pointed at the door. I tried to scream; I want him out! my skin crawled and tears rolled slowly down my cheeks. I felt so violated, I felt disgusting, dirty, and scared. All I could do was pray; I could not speak or advocate for myself. Finally, the therapist told him, "She looks very distraught, you should come back later." I exhaled a sigh of relief as I watched him leave my room.

Unable to communicate my need left me feeling extremely vulnerable. Am I safe? I thought to myself. Will he come back to hurt me? He left looking defeated. From the look in his eyes, he was embarrassed and angry. We were the only people who knew the truth. He hated me, yet here he was pretending I was the love of his life as I sat there fearing for mine... Is this real? I questioned. Would he be coming back, and if he did, would they allow him to just come in? The thought of him being able to charm and joke his way into my personal space, without any truth of who he really was, infuriated me. The more I thought about how casually my abuser was able to walk in and play like we were a happy couple. The angrier I became. I didn't feel safe. I HAD TO GET OUT. I felt like a sitting duck. I knew the consequences of him feeling like I've embarrassed him, in the past, they were often violent and humiliating. I was not ready to add that to my extensive list of problems I had going on. My anxiety was growing by the minute. When my nurse finally came in, I would use a board with different pictures, numbers, and letters. To let her know I wanted my mom. Three simple words (call my mom) that would have taken me less than a second to say in the past, took over an hour of charades, physical strength, and exhaustion, but finally, she understood what I needed. My mom came as soon as possible. After more rounds of charades, asking the nurse, there were a million questions about what happened that day. After trying to understand my complete, shaking, scratch handwriting. She was finally able to piece the story together. My child's father had been up there. They think I wanted him out, but they were unsure. (To this day, I still cannot understand why they were so unsure. In any other setting, a woman crying, shaking her head violently, gesturing towards the door as soon as her "partner" walks in, would have been a series of red flags too intense to ignore. Unfortunately, I would very quickly learn that this would not be the 1st or last time my cries for help would go unnoticed as I searched for answers and navigated the medical system alone as a young black woman. However, it would ultimately deepen my relationship with and dependence on the Lord as I captured glimpses of his miraculous work throughout my journey. In that moment when my abuser was allowed to walk into my room and intimidate me freely, no one batted an eyelash. The next few days were draining. I was so terrified by the thought of being in that position again. The thought of being that vulnerable, that weak, and unable to protect or speak up for myself, I was triggered. The thought of surviving everything I've been through just to be preyed upon disgusted me. This man was playing a game with my mind and my situation, that I could not understand or control.

Ben came back a few days later. Hi, I'm here to see Shabriya Hill. PIN, please, the nurse asked. PIN? What do you mean? He responded, confused.

Do you know the PIN for visitation? Oh no, her mom must have forgotten to give it to me. Can you check with her? I could overhear the conversation taking place behind the glass wall of my room. Anxiety grew deep within me, as fear threatened to freeze me right in my tracks, a boldness, a desire to stop Ben's antics, grew even more. As I frantically pressed on my call button over and over again, the nurse finally came to check on me. Miss Hill, your partner is here to visit. But he doesn't have the PIN. I stared confused. I knew nothing of a PIN and absolutely nothing of any partner. My face, now stoic in anticipation, turned towards her, my eyes locking onto the bright blue eyes in front of me, and I slowly shook my head. No! As I silently prayed that she would listen.

Ok! She made her way back to the front desk. I couldn't help noticing the excitement in her voice as she informed him, he could not visit at this time.

OK. Let me call her mom, he shouted as he left.

Later that night, while resting, I overheard the nurses talking about what had happened. This PIN, which I was unaware of, caused a lot of commotion.

After weeks in the hospital, people outside of my immediate family and friends were learning about what happened. People whom I had just met and family I barely knew were calling the nurses' station and coming to visit. When they learned I was password protected, their shock and mine caused unintentional stress and drama throughout the hospital and family.

"Did you know Kim put a password on Shabriya?"
"Her mom doesn't want us calling!" "So, I can't even call and check on you!?"

It was all so far from the truth.

After Ben's initial unwelcome visit, I struggled through a painful game of charades to explain to my mom what happened. Her face hardened with protective fury. Within hours, she had worked with the hospital staff to create a security system I hadn't known was possible—she put a PIN on me! Anyone visiting would now have to know this confidential code to gain access. No one could see me, call me, or have any contact without first providing this password.

At that moment, I recognized God's hand moving through my mother's actions. Just hours earlier, I had been praying for protection, feeling helpless against Ben's manipulation and the hospital staff's inability to recognize his deception. I hadn't specified how God should answer that prayer—I just knew I needed divine intervention.

Scripture says that God works in mysterious ways, and sometimes the most profound spiritual protection comes through practical human action. My mother, who had once been unable to protect me from my early trauma, was now standing guard like a warrior angel. The same woman I had complicated feelings toward throughout my life had become God's instrument of safety for me.

Finally feeling some sense of ease, knowing that Ben could not just barge in and access me whenever he wanted, I felt my body relax for the first time since awakening. I could finally rest without fear of violation or manipulation. This small measure of security—a simple PIN code—felt like the first piece of solid ground beneath my feet after weeks of treacherous shifting sand.

I missed my daughter, and it was time to be reunited with her after a month that seemed like forever apart.

The prospect of reuniting with my daughter was more than motivation—it was divine fire igniting within me. My love for her and the promise I had made both to her and to God became the engine driving every painful effort toward recovery.

"But those who wait on the LORD shall renew their strength; they shall mount up with wings like eagles, they shall run and not be weary, they shall walk and not faint." (Isaiah 40:31)

"For we walk by faith, not by sight." (2 Corinthians 5:7)

During the next few weeks, I worked with an intensity that surprised even my therapists. I participated in three therapy sessions daily when most patients could barely manage one. In between scheduled therapy, I would laboriously wheel myself around the hospital floor, counting each circuit as a victory. On days when exhaustion seemed to penetrate to my bones, when the medications made even thinking, a challenge, I still pushed through. While lying in my hospital bed during the quiet hours, I performed stretches and exercises the therapists had taught me, determined that not a single hour would be wasted.

This wasn't merely human determination—it was partnership with divine healing. Each movement, painful stretch, and wobbling attempt to stand felt like collaboration between my broken body and God's restorative power. Scripture says, ' I can do all things through Christ who strengthens me' (Philippians 4:13), and I was experiencing the literal truth of those words with every incremental gain.

My doctors had pronounced early verdicts over my life: that I wouldn't survive the brain bleed, that I would never walk again, never speak again. But I had encountered the God who specializes in defying human limitations, who delights in proving medical certainties wrong. His voice within me whispered, 'Keep going,' when everything logical said to accept my limitations.

Prayer became as much a part of my rehabilitation as physical therapy. Before each session, I silently prayed, 'Lord, strengthen what is weak, restore what is broken.' When pain threatened to overwhelm me, I would repeat, 'This suffering is temporary, but Your healing is eternal.' When a milestone seemed impossibly far, I would recall my spiritual journey—how much farther that had been than a few steps across a therapy room.

Every moment of my day, everything that I did, was working towards my getting out of that hospital and getting back to my life. I prayed harder than ever before; my faith was stronger than ever. I knew the Lord was working with me and on me. I woke up from my coma, paralyzed from the waist down, so weak that I could barely lift my head, unable to speak, write, or even hold a PIN on my own. A few weeks later, I was able to stand.

During that time, I also went from trying to talk with a voice box through a hole in my neck to speaking on my own, and even though it wasn't perfect, it was much further than where the doctors told me I would be. My faith and trust in Jesus, coupled with my hard work and determination, took me from the ICU to rehabilitation center within a matter of weeks.

The day of transfer to the rehabilitation center was bittersweet. I was happy to be leaving the hospital, but I would have rather been going home. I tried to talk my doctor into letting me go home and doing therapy there. I tried to tell them that I did not need the center, I was doing great, but they weren't convinced. In my mind, it was like going from prison to jail. Yes, I'm happy to be out of prison, I'm delighted to have fewer restrictions, but I desperately wanted to be free from confinement

Entering the stroke floor of the rehabilitation center was like entering a retirement home.
Every part, including my room, smelled like old people.

I sat through painfully boring, Life Alert meetings. Scanning the room, I was the only 24-year-old and probably the only person under 60. I felt my days were wasted in a place I seemingly did not belong. I rushed through my rehabilitation with only freedom on my mind. Within two weeks, I went from not being able to walk at all to rolling the halls in my wheelchair.

Then, I walked them slowly on my Walker, then with my cane, and finally, just using the rail for assistance as needed. I was done, finished. All the Glory belonged to God; I was in complete awe at the way he partnered with me. The way he lovingly pushed me over the finish line. All that hard work, finally paid off.

Chapter 5

Broken Vessels

The Abandoned Recovery

I was finally home—the goal that had fueled every painful physical therapy session, every speech exercise, every small victory in the hospital. Yet homecoming brought a strange mixture of relief and disorientation. I was happy, yes, but I was undeniably different. The Shabriya who had left for the hospital months ago would never return; in her place stood this new creation—physically altered, spiritually awakened, yet somehow more fragile than before.

"He heals the brokenhearted and binds up their wounds."
(Psalm 147:3)

Physically and mentally, I struggled to navigate this new terrain. The hospital had been structured, with clear objectives and constant support. Home offered freedom but also a profound loneliness I hadn't anticipated. The daily routines that once felt effortless now presented mountainous challenges. Simple tasks like climbing stairs or preparing meals became expeditions requiring strategic planning and immense effort.

In my desperation to escape the hospital, I had focused solely on meeting the discharge requirements, pushing through rehabilitation at a pace that prioritized leaving over healing. I had never truly taken time to acquaint myself with my new reality or mourn what was lost. The spiritual insights and divine presence that had sustained me during my near-death experience seemed to dim in the harsh light of day-to-day struggles.

Scripture speaks of being 'refined in the furnace of affliction' (Isaiah 48:10), but I discovered that refinement doesn't end when the most intense heat subsides.

Sometimes the true testing comes in the cooling, in learning to live with what the fire has forged you to become. I wasn't just recovering from a stroke; I was being reborn into a life I hadn't chosen but now had to embrace.

My mom suggested I come stay at her house, it was less busy and had fewer stairs, but I opted to stay at my grandmother's, where I previously lived. Her home was the security blanket I always reached for. My room was on the top floor, meaning I had to climb four flights of stairs to get there. But I assumed I would have more help because there were more people. My grandmother's home had always been our meeting place. Packed with my cousins, siblings and our friends, since we all lived there at different points within our lives. We hung out there daily and threw parties there almost every weekend. We all knew and loved Mimis, even when she wasn't pleasant. Before my stroke, I had lived there with my grandmother and my daughter Kam, and during my time in the hospital, two of my cousins had moved in.

All my cousins and their friends continued to hang out there. On my first day back, after struggling to navigate the stairs, I called for help, but there was none. I took my time, but by the time I got to the top, I was physically exhausted, my legs hurt, and I was sore. I exhausted so much energy getting to my room, that all I could do was sleep, the rest of the day. The next few days were spent cycling between taking medication and sleeping. I would occasionally get a visitor, a family member, who would come upstairs to check and see how I was doing, and if I felt comfortable enough with them, I would ask them to please bring me something to eat. I was starving.

Before my incident, I did everything, and now there was no one grocery shopping, doing laundry, or cleaning, and I did not have enough energy to keep going to the first floor only to be disappointed. This was before Uber Eats and the Influx of delivery apps, but that wouldn't matter because I did not have money for them anyway. I was unable to work. At 24, my disability wasn't much, and the application for long-term disability was ridiculous for someone in my condition to have to try and navigate and figure it out alone.

All the faith that I had in the community accumulated during my time in the coma slowly started to dwindle day by day as I realized that not only was I incapable of taking care of myself, but that I would not be able to take care of my daughter either. It became increasingly clear that help wasn't coming. No one was coming.

As weeks passed, a chasm grew between my new reality and the unchanged lives surrounding me. My grandmother's home, once a place of belonging, became the stage where I witnessed life continuing without me—a painful theater in which I was neither participant nor even acknowledged spectator.

"I have become a stranger to my brothers, and an alien to my mother's children." (Psalm 69:8)

Each evening brought the familiar sounds of laughter and music from the floor below, where my cousins and their friends gathered to drink, play cards, and escape their daily stresses. The sounds of their normality—of the life I once effortlessly participated in—drifted up through the floorboards like a taunt. I would lie in my bed, immobilized by fatigue and pain, listening to their orders for food delivery, smelling the aromas that never made their way to my room. Hour after hour, I waited, hoping that someone might remember me—might wonder if I too was hungry, might climb those four flights of stairs to check if I needed anything. That moment never came.

In those dark nights, I began to understand the Psalmist's lament: 'I looked for someone to take pity, but there was none; and for comforters, but I found none' (Psalm 69:20). The spiritual abandonment I had feared during my hospital stay had materialized in my own family's home, not through malice but through the casual neglect that is sometimes more wounding than direct rejection.

My hospital room had been filled with professionals paid to care for me. I discovered a deeper loneliness here, surrounded by blood relatives—the isolation of being physically present yet fundamentally unseen. I questioned whether the God who had seemed so near during my crisis had abandoned me in this mundane suffering. Was divine presence reserved only for dramatic medical emergencies but absent in the daily battle to survive neglect and indifference?

Each night became a spiritual desert where I wrestled with these questions, tears soaking my pillow as bass lines thumped through the floor beneath me. In that desert, I was being stripped of illusions about family, recovery, and the nature of healing itself. What I could not yet see was that this stripping away was preparing me for a more authentic relationship with both God and myself—one not dependent on others' validation or care.

I was frustrated and tired of sitting in my room and calling and waiting for help. My stroke left my vocal cords paralyzed and left me unable to speak loudly or raise my voice at all, I was angry that no one thought to turn down the music for even a moment to see if I needed help. I decided to go downstairs and see if there was any food in the kitchen, see if they had left anything. I passed by the room they were in, and the door was closed. I made my way all the way to the kitchen, where my grandmother was sitting at the table. I told her I was really hungry. She told me that they had ordered food and that I should ask them for some, but I refused.

My grandmother shared what she had, I took my portion to my room, so that I could save enough to eat the next day. As I approached the stairs with my walker, I was quickly met with the reality that I could not do it alone.

Standing at the bottom of that staircase, I confronted my new limitations in their starkest form. I tried repeatedly to ascend, each attempt ending in failure, each failure chipping away at the hope I had cultivated during rehabilitation. These weren't hospital stairs with therapists hovering nearby—these were the stairs of my childhood home; a pathway I had traversed thousands of times without thought.

"Though I walk in the midst of trouble, You will revive me; You will stretch out Your hand against the wrath of my enemies, and Your right hand will save me." (Psalm 138:7)

In my frustration, tears began to flow—tears of rage against my broken body, tears of grief for the independence I had lost, tears of disbelief that something as simple as climbing stairs had become an insurmountable obstacle. The food I had managed to scrounge from the kitchen sat mocking me from the step where I had placed it, simultaneously within sight yet beyond reach.

My grandmother witnessed my struggle and responded with the full force of her maternal instinct. She positioned herself at the stairwell and began crying out with a voice that cut through my shame: "Shabriya needs help! Shay-la! Shabriya needs help!" Her elderly voice carried the desperate concern that only a grandmother can embody, a sound that should have pierced any distraction.

What happened next carved a wound deeper than my physical limitations ever could. Rather than rushing to assist, the music volume increased. Laughter grew louder, deliberately drowning out my grandmother's pleas. In that moment, I clearly understood that my family had made a choice—not just to ignore my needs, but to actively reject the responsibility of caring for me.

The humiliation burned hotter than any physical pain I had experienced. I was not merely helpless but deemed unworthy of the minimal effort required to help me ascend stairs. In that moment of profound rejection, I felt closer to Christ's experience in Gethsemane than at any other point in my life—when those He counted on slept while He suffered, when His plea 'Stay here and watch with Me' (Matthew 26:38) went unheeded by those closest to Him.

Yet in the midst of this abandonment, my grandmother's voice represented something profound—a reminder that I was seen by at least one person, that my value didn't de-crease with my ability. Her unsuccessful advocacy became, paradoxically, the catalyst for my determination. If others wouldn't help me, I would find a way to help myself. If family wouldn't rise to meet my needs, I would learn to transcend them.

In the fertile soil of that humiliation, two seeds were planted simultaneously. The first was determination—a God-given resilience that whispered, 'You can overcome this.' The second, growing faster and rooting deeper, was anger—a bitter, choking weed that hissed, 'You're completely alone.' Both began to grow within me, battling for dominance over my heart and mind.

"Let all bitterness, wrath, anger, clamor, and evil speaking be put away from you, with all malice. And be kind to one another, tenderhearted, forgiving one another, even as God in Christ forgave you." (Ephesians 4:31-32)

Scripture warns about the root of bitterness that springs up and causes trouble, defiling many (Hebrews 12:15). I felt this root taking hold, its tendrils wrapping around my thoughts, prayers, and perception of others. My anger wasn't just at my family's indifference—it was at God Himself. Why had He rescued me from death only to abandon me to this humiliation? Why preserve my life if that life would be defined by rejection and isolation?

With these questions burning in my chest, I returned to the kitchen, eyes scanning for anything to help me navigate the stairs. I wasn't thinking clearly; I was operating on pure survival instinct. Moving awkwardly with my walker, I gathered items I thought might help—a broomstick for balance, a bag I could wear across my body to carry food. Through tears and gritted teeth, I formulated a plan.

The ascent was agonizing—physically painful and emotionally excruciating. Each step simultaneously represented a
defeat and a victory. I felt defeated because I shouldn't have
been climbing these stairs alone, and I felt victory because
I was proving to myself that I could survive abandonment.
When I finally reached the top landing, sweat-soaked and
trembling with exertion, I turned back to see my grandmother standing at the bottom, still calling for help that
wouldn't come.

When someone finally appeared, responding to Mimi's
persistent calls with an irritated "OK, what do you want?
" I had already passed through a point of no return in my
heart. 'I decided I didn't need their help,' I told myself,
the words becoming a mantra of forced independence. 'I
don't need anyone's help.' The declaration felt empowering
in the moment, but I couldn't yet see how it contradicted
everything I had learned during my spiritual journey—that
human interdependence reflects God's design, that needing
others isn't weakness but the natural state of being created
for community.

This moment of rejection became the soil where my anger
and self-reliance grew together, twisted around each other
like vines—impossible to separate, each feeding the other.
What I couldn't recognize then was that my determination
to survive without help was my greatest strength and my
most dangerous vulnerability.

A devastating realization washed over me as I finally
reached my room and collapsed onto my bed. These same
people—these cousins now partying beneath me—had
gathered around what they believed was my deathbed just
weeks earlier. They had cried tears that seemed genuine,
spoken words of love and concern, and prayed for my

recovery with apparent sincerity. The contrast between their hospital vigil and their current indifference created cognitive dissonance I couldn't reconcile.

"It is better to trust in the LORD than to put confidence in man." (Psalm 118:8)

The individuals I had consistently prioritized, for whom I had sacrificed and served throughout my life, couldn't be bothered to climb a staircase to check if I had eaten. All those years of going out of my way, being everyone's emotional support, and putting family above all else—none of it translated into reciprocal care when I became the one in need.

This wasn't just disappointment; it was the shattering of my entire framework for understanding human relationships. The concept of 'family', "Family Over Everything" that had once anchored me—even through difficult times with my mother—suddenly seemed like an elaborate fiction. The love I believed defined these relationships revealed itself as conditional, present only when it required nothing in return.

The spiritual implications were even more profound. During my near-death experience, I encountered divine love—unconditional, all-encompassing, perfectly attuned to my needs. I returned to earth carrying that standard of love within me, only to confront its stark absence in my most intimate human connections. How could I reconcile these realities? If God's love flowed through people, why was it so absent in those closest to me?

I remembered Job's lament: 'My relatives have failed me, my close friends have forgotten me' (Job 19:14). Like Job, I was discovering that human loyalty often vanishes when tested by inconvenience. The pain of this realization cut deeper than any physical wound, creating a spiritual hemorrhage that threatened the faith I had cultivated during my hospital stay.

Yet even in this moment of bitter recognition, a strange seed of gratitude began to germinate alongside my anger. There was a harsh gift in this truth—the gift of seeing clearly what had always been present but hidden. 'It hurt, but I appreciated it,' I thought to myself, recognizing that illusions stripped away, however painfully, create space for authentic understanding.

What I couldn't yet see was that this disillusionment with human love was preparing me to depend more fully on divine love—that sometimes God allows human supports to fail so that we discover His unfailing presence. The lesson would take years to learn fully, but its first painful teachings began that night in my solitary room.

The following week, my mom started checking in on me frequently. I appreciated it; at first, I thought she was genuinely concerned about my well-being. I told her I was having a difficult time, and she explained to me that I needed to get my act together so that I could take care of my child. She convinced me that it was better for my 2yearold daughter to be with me in the state I was in because of how much she missed me, and that I needed to be a mother and take care of my daughter. I agreed and asked her to bring Kam home.

Within the first 48 hours, I knew I had made a mistake; I was not equipped to care for a 2-year-old. I could barely take care of myself. The patience that I once had to deal with things, the small things that all children do, I no longer possessed. I was on so much medication that I was tired and slept most of the day. I had become so depressed that I could barely get out of my bed. I began to experience severe migraines and pains in my brain that the doctors continuously tried to convince me were normal, but deep within me, I knew it was something more. With that pain came this lingering fear that I would die in my sleep, and my 2-year-old daughter would wake up to my dead body, so I never slept at night. I would sit up all night, every night, praying to the Lord, keep me throughout the night, and if it were his will that I must go, my daughter wouldn't be the one to find me. This was my prayer every day for the next year.

A weekend into it, I admitted the devastating truth—I couldn't care for my daughter. The realization crushed me. With my hands shaking and throat tight, I called my mom, something I never wanted to do. Tears streamed down my face as I confessed my helplessness.

"Mom, please," I sobbed, my voice breaking. "Something's wrong with me. I'm not myself. I'm afraid I'm going to die. It's not safe for Kam to be with me." The words caught in my throat. "I think I'm depressed."

The term felt foreign on my tongue. We had never discussed depression, anxiety, or suicidal thoughts in our family. These were weaknesses we didn't acknowledge, demons we didn't name.

"You're overreacting," she dismissed. "Kam will be fine. Just have a drink and calm down."

I pleaded harder, desperation making my voice raw. My mom had always helped with my sister's son when she was partying or being irresponsible. Surely, she would understand that my situation—my inability to function— was beyond my control. Surely, she would see that I wasn't choosing this.

"Please," I begged, "just take her for a little while."

"No."

That single word demolished my last hope. I cried silently into the phone, utterly lost. What was I going to do? What could I do? I had no options, no solutions, nowhere to turn.

I swallowed my devastation, making excuses for her refusal. It was my fault, after all. She'd already cared for my daughter for over a month during my hospitalization. I should be fine now. I don't need help, I can handle this alone.

Following her advice, I poured myself a drink. The alcohol seemed to soften the edges of my despair, so I poured another.

I stumbled to bed, and for the first time in months, I fell asleep without crying, staying up all night, or sitting in darkness and fear. I thought my mom had given me the key to getting through, or at least through the night.

Monday came, and so did another doctor's appointment. Ben, who had been conveniently using my short and long term memory loss to once again play the role of the devoted partner, picked us up to take me to my appointment and watch Kam while I was there. Between physical therapy, speech therapy, neurology appointments, and general medicine appointments, it felt like I was always at the doctor's office. It felt like I was there just as much as I had been while in the hospital, so I was just grateful to have his help.

As he opened the door and reached toward me to help me get out, a flashback hit me like a ton of bricks — of him hitting me in the face. Shocked, I looked at him with fear and confusion.

"What's wrong?" He asked, sensing my hesitation. "Nothing, I got it." I responded, annoyed. Who was this man, I thought to myself? I tried to remember, but the memories were gone. I spent the entire hour of physical therapy and the days to come, trying to figure out what was real. He came to pick me up, and I decided to try and let it go. I had no one else, there was no one to help, and no reason to make things more difficult than they already were. At least he was helping, I thought to myself.

As I searched around for true joy, my daughter was the only one there. At the age of 2, she became the only thing that kept me going, the only thing I lived for. She was my only source of happiness, yet she was gone with her dad who had fought me for joint custody before any of this happened. I made the mistake of letting Ben know just how much Kam kept me going. So, when my memories began to come back and I stopped allowing him to deceive me and everyone else, I stood firm on my decision to just co-parent Kam without any romantic relationship. I was met with anger and threats to use my circumstances to take our daughter completely away from me. He used the court and my love for her as a weapon to control me and keep me in fear. My temporary joy would turn to sadness every time I watched her leave. During those times, whenever I needed to feel better, I reached for another bottle of tequila. Tequila: my remedy, my solace. We quickly became best friends. My life had changed so much; I was so lonely. Alcohol quickly became my outlet, my comfort. Night after night, I stayed up drinking my problems away.

As I searched for answers for my continued physical pain, I asked my Dr. for a CAT Scan of my brain, to ensure everything had healed and the inflammation reduced properly after my brain surgery. He refused, stating that I had already been tested when I was discharged from the hospital several months prior, He continued to tell me that I was "overreacting" and "Nothing is wrong." Leaving me without any answers or even acknowledgment of the excruciating pain I was still suffering with. This, ongoing frustration with not being heard by my medical professionals—people who are supposed to help me— made me feel ignored and insignificant. Leaving me no choice but to endure the pain. He offered me Oxycontin as a consolation prize, I never asked for. One evening as I searched for something to ease my unbearable pain. I decided I would give this new pain medication a try. Instantly I felt my body weighing down, my grandmother screamed as I leaned over falling asleep mid-sentence, during a conversation. Resembling the junkie addicts I skipped passed while walking to the store as a child. Shabriya! Her screams just barely piercing my eardrums, just enough to make me aware of what was happening. The urgency in her voice hinted that I needed to lay down fast, but my body would barely move. What the Hell did he give me?! I was pissed, why would anyone knowingly give out a medication like that? I challenged him. Questioning why he refused to give me the pain medication I had used just fine, to turn around and give me what I considered, dope. Why would you give me something strong enough to have me nodding off while standing up, like I'm a dope fiend! What's your problem? Questions that I demanded answers to but only left the Dr. angry that I had the nerve to question him. Which resulted in me being accused and flagged for "drug seeking." I did not understand why the highly addictive drugs were being pushed on me like Skittles that I kept saying I did not want, yet the less addictive medication that actually helped was being treated like dope. I didn't want to be high, I just wanted to be comfortable enough to make it through the day. Now I was unable to receive any pain medication at all, my anger and frustration continued to grow. The unfair treatment, the pain, the daily struggles were wearing me down day by day. Each day, seemingly worse than the last. I continued, consistently praying and hoping that I would make it to the next day. Most days, I only get a few hours of sleep, if any. Sometimes, I would go days without sleep, waiting until my daughter was scheduled to be with her dad just to get some rest, knowing that at least if something did happen, she wouldn't be there to find me or witness this. This went on for a year, until I could finally retake my scans and test only because it was mandatory for me to have yearly testing. I anxiously awaited this day, knowing everything I had been claiming to my doctors, my pleas that "something is wrong!" My year long suffering, all the answers relied on the results of this test. I fasted for 12 hours and waited to be called forever. Finally, they called me back and prepped me for my angiogram. For the next three hours, I sat in discomfort as they pushed dye through my arteries, trying to find any issues.

"Alright, Ms. Hill, we're almost done, and we'll get you out of here soon. " I tried to hold back tears as I realized I would be rushed out and ignored again for another year. In that moment, I called on God and silently prayed. Lord, this has been a journey, and you have blessed me so much. God, please, I need you. If something is wrong, they must find it. Please, I can't do this for another year, Lord." I pleaded.

"Ok, Ms. Hill, the last one. Where are we? Wait, go back."

My heart dropped. "Release. Right there, do you see that?" The energy in the room shifted. "Capture that right there." Tears started to flow down my face unexpectedly. I knew God intervened at the very last second when we all thought it was over. I didn't know how; I didn't understand; I didn't care. "Thank you, Jesus! I proclaimed. At that moment, I was not aware of how serious my situation was. I was just incredibly grateful that God confirmed what I had sensed, even without the Dr. confirming it. However, something was still pressing on my mind. What did they find?

"Okay, Ms. Hill, we will take you to the recovery area."

I was rushed off to meet with my neurosurgeon. "Okay, we have your test results, and we know why you had a brain bleed." "Whew, finally! That's great." I said excited. "Well, you have something called Arteriovenous malformation (AVM)." "What's that?" "Your arteries and veins move blood throughout your body. Yours are tangled up like a knot, at the back of your brain. Stress or pressure can cause it to burst or bleed, which is what we now believe hap-pened to you when you experienced your bleed." "Huh." I didn't understand what he was talking about. He replied, "You've been walking around like a ticking time bomb," he chuckled. I thought back to all the times I felt stressed, how my brain would start to hurt when I got angry, and when my blood pressure would rise. I recalled all the times I told my doctors something was wrong. I cried, I begged, I pleaded, and I was ignored. And now he was sitting here laughing at the fact that I've spent the last year of my life like a "ticking time bomb." My anger grew, but I said nothing. After all, he was the best brain surgeon in the city, one of the best in the world— I wouldn't let my anger ruin my chance at getting this fixed. I exhaled, remained calm, put on a smile that made him comfortable, and continued to listen. He was my surgeon, and I didn't want to make him uncomfortable by correcting him. But that thought lingered for so long; to think back to any of those moments, out of the hundreds, maybe even thousands of times throughout the year, I could've died and no one took me seriously. I finally felt validated, but also invisible. This reinstated my deep mistrust in the medical system and healthcare professionals concerning my care.

"Ok, so what's next?"
"You'll need to have emergency surgery. But I'll be out of town for a few weeks, so how about next month?" "Is that safe?" I questioned, emergency surgery sounding like something that needed intervention right away. I'm not too worried; you've made it this long.

Each of his responses added fuel to my irritation. Who tells someone they're walking around like a ticking time bomb, I thought.

I could die at any moment... but he'll do the emergency surgery weeks later? I silently questioned to myself. "OK", sounds good. I confirmed

The day of surgery arrived. This time was different because it was scheduled, planned, and I supposedly knew what would happen. My surgeon said I would be out within three days. A week later, I was still in pain and still in the hospital; I could barely lift my head. I called my nurse for my pain meds, and as soon as she came in, I felt the energy shift. I couldn't have the lights on; they burned my eyes. She tried to turn them on anyway, despite my pleas for her to turn them off; she responded coldly, telling me I shouldn't still need medication and that I should be out of the hospital by now. I replied, "This is my second brain surgery in less than a year. How are you going to tell me how my body should respond?"

"Well, I've had six brain surgeries and have never had any trouble! " She fired back.

"OK, well that's good for you, but what does that have to do with me?" I couldn't believe my nurse was treating me like this. I told her you have a horrible attitude before asking her to leave. She was so focused on going back and forth with me, trying to prove a point, that she did not even realize or care that she was adding to my pain and discomfort. I was once again lying in the hospital, vulnerable in excruciating pain, trying and failing to advocate for myself. As my nurse, I trusted her to care for my needs, and here I was being belittled, berated, and attacked again. My whispers for the manager went unheard, but I suddenly gained the strength to demand that she leave and never come back, boldly. I called for her manager with a voice that commanded attention, one that had been gone all year. I would usually ignore being mistreated, anxiety threatened to overwhelm me at the very thought of confrontation, but I couldn't let this go. It didn't sit right with me. I was so angry. Why was I being treated like this, and where was God in all of it?"

At this point it had been a year since my stroke, I was sharing my testimony with anyone who would listen. I would speak confidently about being in the presence of God. I did not have the vocabulary to explain the fullness of what happened. I just knew God was real. My boldness in telling what I experienced got me back lash I couldn't understand. People I never met hated me and treated me like trash, everyone including those closest to me labeled me crazy. Crazy for an encounter I knew was real. My encounter was written off as a trauma induced dream, the medical explanations, and everyone tearing down what I had gone through coupled with confusion of why God would continue to allow me to suffer, made me question myself. Was it all a dream? Something deep down inside me knew it was real, but I decided that I would keep it to myself, sharing only with people I deemed "safe" or not at all.

"Be sober-minded; be watchful. Your adversary, the devil, prowls around like a roaring lion, seeking someone to devour. Resist him, firm in your faith, knowing that your brotherhood is experiencing the same kinds of suffering worldwide." - 1 Peter 5:8-9

"Kill yourself", I heard in my ear loud and clear. I was confused. All these months in recovery, after my second brain trauma, I had been asked millions of times if I was having any suicidal thoughts, almost as if I was expected to after everything, I had experienced. No, I would respond, curious yet somewhat annoyed about the excessive number of times they would ask.

Was this happening now? This wasn't what I expected a suicidal thought to be; it was more of a demand than a thought. You kill yourself. I shouted back. Before reminding myself, I was driving home alone. What was that, I thought? To myself, while questioning my reality. I could still feel the warmth and the wetness of the breath of whatever was talking to me. A confession that this was very real... Suddenly, I had a rush of thoughts and emotions wanting to slam my car into the concrete wall ahead of me. The thoughts of this thing that was separate from me now mingled with mine, further making me question my reality. I inhaled slowly and exhaled deeply as I whispered to my-

self. F#%k, I'm finally losing it. AHHHHHH, I screamed
in frustration, heart racing. I hurried home and into my bed.
Something shifted that day. I felt the weight of the world
and sadness crushing down onto my shoulders. A darkness
and energy I had never felt before. It didn't just feel like
sadness; it felt like emptiness. Thoughts of shame and doubt
slowly filled my mind and spilled over into every inch of
my being.

What's happening? I wondered to myself, while crying
about how crazy I felt. I went to bed hoping it would go
away, but when I woke up, it was there again, whispering,
"You should have died; you don't deserve to be here. Kam
would be better off." thoughts about how no one loved me
and how "my mom has always hated me" filled my mind.
Lies that began to feel like the truth, and the more I tried
to ignore them, the louder they grew. Day in and day out,
this voice was punching me down until I couldn't take it
anymore. The thoughts were becoming more vivid; everything had become so intense. Throughout all I had been
through, I had not opened a Bible—not once. I didn't feel it
was essential to a relationship with God; I assumed prayer
and brief moments at church were enough. Looking back,
I was face to face with the forces of evil again yet still had
no clue how to fight.

"For our struggle is not against flesh and blood, but against
the rulers, against the authorities, against the powers of this
dark world and the spiritual forces of evil in the heavenly
realms." (Ephesians 6:12)

I was spiritually naked, possessing not a single piece of the
armor of God. No belt of truth, no breastplate of righteousness, no gospel of peace, no shield of faith to extinguish
the enemy's flaming arrows, no helmet of salvation, and

no sword of the Spirit, which is the word of God. I stood unprotected on a battlefield I didn't even recognize.

I tried to reach out to my family for help, even turning to the church to share what I was experiencing. But even after all we endured, the discussion of mental health and depression or any topic from the past were all off limits. I knew no one—not a single friend or family member—who was truly submitted to Christ, which meant spiritual warfare would never enter the conversation. Even after my near-death experience, I struggled to connect with my family or feel comfortable being vulnerable with them.

As my fear grew about what might happen to me, overwhelmed by sadness and isolation, I made one last attempt to understand my reality. I approached my sister, starting carefully with questions about our mom.

"How was Mom while we were growing up?" I asked, my voice trembling slightly. The memories flooding back painted a picture vastly different from what I witnessed now, and I didn't know what to trust anymore.

"What do you mean?" she asked defensively.

"Like, how was she? Were we close?" I pressed, desperate for confirmation.

"Shabriya, why are you asking me this?" she snapped, annoyed.

I swallowed hard. "I'm asking because you know I've lost many of my memories, and as they return..." My voice cracked. I don't have many memories of her being a mother. Nothing showing us affection, nothing that feels like love."

"Don't start this nonsense!" she screamed, her reaction only confirming my fears.

"Please," I begged, tears welling in my eyes. "I just need to know. Did she even love us? I'm trying to understand why she doesn't feel like my mom."

The desperation in my voice hung in the air between us.

"Bye, Shabriya. I'm not doing this," she said coldly. "She was a great mom."

"Please," I whispered as she walked away, leaving me with my unanswered questions and growing dread. The rejection cut deep; another door slammed in my face when I needed connection most.

I ran to my room, heartbroken. I just wanted to feel like the people around me were a safe space. Even if I couldn't remember, I had no loving family memories with them, and as a mother, I couldn't imagine my daughter feeling that way about me. Seeking comfort, I made myself a drink and then several more. I tried to numb the pain, tried to numb the voices. I didn't want to feel anything, but the pain wouldn't go away. I needed help, I wanted help. I asked for help. But no one would help me.

Learning to Walk Again

I woke up crying; the voices were right. I should be dead. I was tired of fighting. I remembered how God brought me this far; I couldn't just give up. I decided to reach out for help. I searched for mental health services, but they were all too expensive, and I was still fighting to get my longterm disability approved. My state medical didn't cover or offer anything. I decided to narrow it down to affordable mental health services. I found a community crisis center, and I just dropped in, as I had been crying for hours nonstop. I went in crying, "Please help me, please." The front desk person responded, "I'll get someone immediately."

"Are you okay?"
"I don't know," I replied, breathing heavily.
"You can wait in this room until I can get someone to come down."
When that someone finally arrived, I was on the floor, tears streaming down my face until it felt raw and swollen. I was hyperventilating and couldn't catch my breath. I was on the floor in the fetal position, afraid that I had no idea what was wrong and no way to control it.
I had so many years of tears that I never cried because I didn't want to be seen as weak. I painted this picture of a strong Black woman that I was subconsciously always trying to live up to. " You're so strong, you're so resilient! " Seemingly compliments, that I heard every time I talked about what I was going through, that I would later grow to hate.

Yes, I was strong, and yes, I'm a Black woman, but something about hearing those words strung together made everything I was going through feel dismissed. It meant that I had learned to navigate trauma so well (or at least pretended to) that I was now undeserving of or did not need help. It meant I was capable of withstanding what other women were not. It meant no one was coming to save me. In that moment, in my mind, it all came crumbling down; every tear I had never cried was coming out at once, and nothing could be done to stop it. I put my cape on for everyone else all my life, and now no one is coming for me. I thought to myself as I saw a glimpse of light pushing into the closet's darkness, where I broke down. Hello...? The whisper of a stranger. The psychiatrist, gently pushing the door open to allow the light in, was more than just an answer to my cries for help; it was a reflection of God's grace.

Finding Strength in Weakness

I have told you these things so you may have peace in me. In this world, you will have trouble. But take heart! I have overcome the world." (John 16:33)

They set me up with a team: a counselor, NP, and psychiatrist. I received the help and support I so desperately needed. I felt seen and heard instead of being brushed off or treated as crazy. They would offer me ongoing support for years after. This was just a small step in the transformative story that God was writing, and it was exactly what I needed at the time.

Feeling hopeful about finally receiving mental health services, I began my search for spiritual care and community.

Lisa had been my sister for twenty years in every way but blood. As my daughter's godmother and my closest confidante, she was the one person I thought would never abandon me.

After my stroke, I looked to her for spiritual guidance, believing her daily church attendance meant she knew God better than I did. She brought me to her church, where I hoped to find community during my darkest time. Instead, I received only a perfunctory prayer when I bared my soul about depression despite God's miracle in saving my life. "Is that it?" I asked, my disappointment crushing the hope I had in the church's spiritual intervention. Church wasn't the sanctuary I'd expected, but she continued to encourage me to come along.

Until one day, I loyally warned her about her boyfriend's lies. I had confirmed he was living a double life and watching him play in her face and say nothing felt wrong. We cried together as I revealed the truth, and I comforted her through her heartbreak. Weeks later, she suddenly cut all contact. After three agonizing weeks of self-blame and unanswered messages, her reason stunned me: I had suggested fresh green beans instead of canned ones for her father's dinner. I was apologetic though I knew that couldn't be reason. As she continued the truth became clear.

The revelation was devastating—twenty years wasted over something so trivial. The truth crashed down—she had never seen me as an equal but as her "ratchet ghetto friend," her entertainment. Our friendship was just a charade, with her as the "rich," popular girl and me as the struggling sidekick. She had been spinning false narratives about me and our friendship since High school, maybe even longer. I never even realized it until that moment and the revelation hit me hard. Hurt and disappointed I wanted to go off on her. She never cared. As anger slowly threatened to consume me. I heard a soft whisper, "Don't do it. She's counting on you responding that way." Fighting my tears I grabbed Kam and left.

This rejection during my recovery intensified my anger and isolation. I was losing friends and family, left and right. My once close circle, dropping like flies. Yet another person I'd trusted and prioritized had proven my value to them was negligible, leaving me more alone than ever.

Too often we come to Christ (or hear stories of people coming to Christ) and align ourselves with individuals and churches that claim to be Christian without first testing their "fruit." When these relationships fail to produce good fruit, they end in trauma, disappointment, hurt, and pain. It's easy to allow our experiences with trusted individuals turn us away from church, community, and even from Jesus. Sometimes it can seem easier to place blame on the church as a whole, than to place blame on the individuals misrepresenting it. "It is not good for man to be alone" is more than a revelation about man and wife; it is recognition that God never intended for us to do life by ourselves. So, do not be deceived into loneliness and isolation. Do not look to the Sunday "Christians" or to people like the Pharisees, who try to enforce religious law. Instead with the guidance of the Holy Spirit seek wise Christian community, ones that are overflowing with "good fruit" and prepare to be loved and sharpened!

"For the entire law is fulfilled in keeping this one command: "Love your neighbor as yourself."
(Galatians 5:14)

"As iron sharpens iron, so one person sharpens another." (Proverbs 27:17)

Chapter 6
Deceptions

The Price of Perfection

After being pushed away by my sister, dismissed at church, and then rejected by my best friend of two decades, isolation became more than an emotional state—it was my daily reality. The walls of my room seemed to close in around me; each rejection having stripped away another layer of the "protective" community I once took for granted.

One evening, after tucking Kam into bed, the weight of my aloneness became unbearable. I sank to my knees beside my bed—a posture of prayer my body remembered from childhood but that my adult life had largely abandoned. The tears came without warning, hot and urgent, years of stored grief finding release. My daughter joined me.

"Delight yourself also in the LORD, and He shall give you the desires of your heart." (Psalm 37:4)

"Please," I whispered, my voice breaking, "send me someone to love me well. Please send someone who will be there for me, Lord." The prayer was raw, unfiltered by theological correctness or spiritual sophistication. It was the cry of a wounded heart that had tried self-sufficiency and found it wanting. "This person has to be someone who maybe knew me from the past," I added, "so they'll understand who I was before I had my stroke and all these problems."

As the words left my lips, I felt a twinge of doubt. Was I treating God like a cosmic dating service? Was this prayer legitimate or merely desperation masked as spiritual seeking? Scripture tells us to cast our cares upon Him because He cares for us (1 Peter 5:7), but did that extend to romantic loneliness? In my heart, I questioned whether God concerned Himself with such matters, even as I asked.

"Yes, this was my real prayer," I thought with embarrassment and sincerity, hoping he would answer it. I didn't know if my request aligned with His purposes or if He was even listening to someone whose faith journey had been as inconsistent as mine. Yet Scripture promises that the Lord is near to the brokenhearted (Psalm 34:18), and in that moment, I qualified, if nothing else.

A couple of weeks later—that timeframe itself neither too immediate to seem coincidental nor too delayed to appear disconnected from my prayer—I received a dm. The name immediately triggered high school memories: Drew, a classmate who had briefly dated my now ex-best friend during our first year. He had never captured my attention then; our social circles had intersected without my giving him a second glance.

"Beloved, do not believe every spirit, but test the spirits, whether they are of God." (1 John 4:1)

As I stared at his message, a strange mixture of emotions stirred. Was this God's answer to my prayer? The timing seemed too perfect to dismiss entirely, yet imperfect to claim with certainty. Scripture speaks of God giving us the desires of our hearts (Psalm 37:4), but it also warns about testing every spirit (1 John 4:1). Which was this—divine provision or dangerous distraction?

Feeling lonely and bored, desperate for connection yet wary of disappointment, I rationalized the potential connection. "He was a jock in school, tall and handsome, someone many girls liked," I reminded myself, mentally cataloging qualities that might matter to others, if not to me. "He wasn't my type then, but surely after all these years, he must have grown and changed. We all have."

I hovered my finger over his message, Scripture and doubt battling in my mind. "Ask and it will be given to you; seek and you will find; knock and the door will be opened to you" (Matthew 7:7) whispered one voice. "Be careful what you pray for," cautioned another.

" I might be opening a can of worms, but why not just take a risk and deal with the consequences?" I finally reasoned; a metaphor more prophetic than I could have known then. There was something almost predestined in how quickly I dismissed my reservations—as though the divine script had already been written, including my initial hesitation and subsequent surrender.

Looking back, I can see how this moment embodied the mysterious intersection of God's sovereignty and human free will—how answers to prayer often come packaged in ways that require our discernment rather than mere acceptance. The question wasn't simply whether Drew was God-sent, but whether I had the spiritual wisdom to navigate what his arrival in my life would mean.

Our relationship began with an intoxicating intensity that felt like divine confirmation. Drinking, laughing, talking for hours, and sharing physical intimacy created a passionate beginning, validating my prayer for connection. We fell into each other's lives with an ease that felt predetermined, two puzzle pieces somehow separated until this perfect moment of alignment.

"Do not be unequally yoked together with unbelievers. For what fellowship has righteousness with lawlessness?" (2 Corinthians 6:14)

Months later, my therapist would give this connection a clinical name: trauma bonding. The term cut through my romantic interpretation, illuminating a psychological framework and diminishing what we shared. We had both weathered significant storms—my stroke and recovery, his own undisclosed wounds—creating a shared understanding of brokenness that normal relationships couldn't match. We were always ready to escape reality together, to create moments of pleasure that temporarily masked our pain.

What my therapist couldn't address—and what I struggled to discern myself—was the spiritual dimension of this connection. Scripture warns that "Satan himself masquerades as an angel of light" (2 Corinthians 11:14), suggesting that not everything that feels divinely orchestrated actually originates from God. The comfort and connection I found with Drew felt like answers to prayer, yet the methods we used to escape reality—alcohol, physical pleasure, constant distraction—contradicted the spiritual healing I claimed to seek.

The good times between us burned bright but brief, like matches struck in darkness—momentarily blinding, quickly extinguished. Drew possessed a remarkable talent for creating the illusion of permanence, for making each fleeting joy feel like the foundation of something lasting. I desperately wanted to believe in the stability he projected that I overlooked the evidence of its fragility.

Behind my conscious thoughts ran a troubling question I dared not articulate: Had God answered my prayer with exactly what I had asked for rather than what I needed? Scripture recounts how the Israelites demanded meat in the wilderness, and God granted their request while sending "leanness into their soul" (Psalm 106:15). Was this relationship similarly my demanded provision—technically an answer to prayer but not aligned with divine purpose for my healing and growth?

These questions remained unasked as I surrendered to the temporary comfort of being wanted, held, and seen—even if what was seen wasn't my complete self but merely the version Drew desired to see.

We quickly became inseparable, our lives merging with the eager intensity of those who have known profound loneliness. Every moment apart felt like unnecessary separation, and every hour together reinforced our connection. He made me feel wanted in ways that healed the raw wounds left by family abandonment and friendship betrayal. For the first time since my stroke, I no longer felt fundamentally alone. In many ways, he appeared to be exactly what I had prayed for—a connection to my past who understood my present, someone who chose to be with me when others had walked away.

"Though one may be overpowered by another, two can withstand him. And a threefold cord is not quickly broken." (Ecclesiastes 4:12)

Yet beneath this apparent answer to prayer lurked a troubling imbalance. Months into our relationship, he still refused to make our connection "official." We existed in that modern relational purgatory called a "situationship"— enjoying the benefits of a committed partnership without the security of acknowledged commitment. Meanwhile, I gave him everything a woman could offer a man: passionate love, physical intimacy, home-cooked meals, a clean space, thoughtful gifts, and genuine affection for his children. I integrated myself into his family while he enjoyed my benefits.

This imbalance reflected a spiritual truth I wasn't yet ready to confront: human relationships often mirror our relationship with God. Just as I gave Drew my full devotion while receiving conditional commitment in return, I had often approached God with similar disparity—seeking His blessings and protection while hesitating to surrender my life to His purposes fully. Scripture describes God as a jealous God (Exodus 20:5) who seeks wholehearted commitment, not mere association. Was this situationship teaching me, through painful object lesson, about the nature of covenant versus convenience?

Each time Drew deflected discussions about our future, each time he accepted my nurturing without offering security in return, a small voice within me whispered that perhaps this wasn't God's provision but rather a mirror reflecting my own spiritual inconsistency back to me. The voice grew louder as my emotional investment deepened without his corresponding commitment, but I silenced it repeatedly, unwilling to surrender the connection I had convinced myself was divinely orchestrated.

"What are we?" I finally asked one evening, the question hanging between us like a suspended weight. The words emerged from curiosity and spiritual exhaustion—from the constant labor of convincing myself that uncertainty was God's will for my life.

"For I know the thoughts that I think toward you, says the LORD, thoughts of peace and not of evil, to give you a future and a hope." (Jeremiah 29:11)

"I need you to decide," I continued, finding courage in desperation. "You don't need six months to know if you want me to be your girl. It's not like we're getting married."

The distinction felt important—I wasn't asking for lifetime commitment, merely acknowledgment of what already existed between us.

He shifted uncomfortably, eyes darting anywhere but my face. The silence stretched between us, a canvas on which I projected all my fears about unworthiness and abandonment. In that silent moment, I felt God's presence more clearly than I had in months—not in burning bush certainty, but in the quiet conviction that I deserved clarity, that divine love never keeps us guessing about where we stand.

"I can't keep doing all this for someone who doesn't want to be committed to me," I finally said, the words emerging with a spiritual authority that surprised even me. "I look crazy." The admission carried a double meaning—crazy to others observing our relationship, but also to myself, to the God who had watched me settle for less than covenant love.

"Shabriya, I want you," he replied with practiced sincerity. "I don't want to disappoint you."

"Then don't," I said simply, using both the ultimatum and invitation statements.

Shortly after we decided to be exclusive—his reluctant concession more than enthusiastic embrace. My psychiatrist referred me to a residential treatment facility, in an attempt to get my depression and negative thoughts under control. I had been honest with Drew about my stroke and depression during my recovery, and he never judged me. He even stood by me during my stay in treatment, and I finally felt seen and supported, even though I hadn't been frank about the severity of my condition and my constant suicidal thoughts and ideations.

The timing felt significant, as though God were simultaneously opening two doors in my life: one through this relationship, another through this new path toward healing. In the moment, I couldn't discern which door led to genuine restoration and which might lead to further wounding. Scripture tells us that God works all things together for good for those who love Him (Romans 8:28), but it doesn't promise that every path feels good in the moment.

The reluctant label of "exclusive" brought temporary relief but not the security I had prayed for. Even as I celebrated this small victory in my relationship with Drew, a quiet voice reminded me that God never hesitates to claim us as His own, never requires ultimatums to acknowledge His love for us. The contrast between divine certainty and human hesitation created a dissonance I wasn't yet ready to hear fully, but its melody had begun to play in the background of my heart.

My short-term stay in the treatment facility brought me relief as well, though not in the way I expected, since my relief did not come from the medication or the mandatory group therapy sessions. As I scanned yet another room, feeling as if I did not belong, I quickly realized that many of us were battling demons we lacked the knowledge to properly name. Yes, some were truly having an extremely challenging time, struggling with their mental health and medication did help them, but others were battling something much bigger, darker, manifesting right in front of our eyes, spewing hatred for no reason, randomly citing scripture, shifting from seemingly pleasant to evil, taunting me, every time I entered a room. "I don't know why she acts like that towards you, she's always so sweet" I was told constantly but something deep inside me recognized the truth. "Oh, these are real demons," I said to myself, shocked because it was something I only heard about in stories told by friends from foreign countries and would occasionally read in the Bible as a child. My relief came in the understanding of the truth that laid in those Bible verses, this was worldly confirmation outside of myself, a larger battle between light and darkness. I was not afraid; somehow, I knew God was with me even though His presence felt far. I was, however, highly annoyed. At the time, I still didn't understand warfare or deliverance. All I knew was that God was protecting me. Yet I would still question, how did I get here?

After all the medication, I was turning into a shell of my former self; nothing changed, and depression and suicidal thoughts continued to worsen. This would eventually end once I began to truly live for Christ, submitting everything onto him partnered with continued therapy and even medication when needed. I have been able to receive forgiveness, deliverance and healing, claiming victory over depression and suicidal ideations. I am not against medication; I know it can be helpful. If I have a season where I need medication, I take it, but now it actually works, I make progress and come off it. But now knowing the truth, I understand it was a battle I could not win alone. I had to actively invite God in, truly seek Him instead of just wandering where He was. Even these darkest moments, all give glory to God.

False Promises in Miami

After my stroke and the resulting cascade of medications, my body became yet another aspect of my life beyond my control. My weight fluctuated dramatically—up and down in ways that seemed to mock my attempts at stability. I began to obsess over my appearance, scrutinizing every change in the mirror, each fluctuation becoming evidence of my failure to recover 'properly.' My self-esteem, which had never been robust, plummeted to depths I hadn't known possible.

> *"I praise you because I am fearfully and wonderfully made; your works are wonderful, I know that full well."*
> (Psalm 139:14)

The truth was, I had never truly felt beautiful. Growing up with a mother who used words like weapons—'B*#@h! Ugly, fat, dumb—had planted seeds of self-hatred that had grown into mighty oaks over the decades. But this poststroke insecurity was different—more intense, more desperate, more consuming. I had stared death in the face, experienced spiritual realms beyond the physical, only to return to a body that felt increasingly alien to me.

After months of dating a man every local female wanted, comparison became my constant companion. I watched how other women looked at him, how his eyes sometimes lingered on certain bodies, and I began to measure myself against an impossible standard. Despite my spiritual awakening during my stroke, I had failed to integrate its most profound lesson: that my worth transcended my physical form, that I was 'fearfully and wonderfully made' by divine design.

Instead, I became obsessed with 'glowing up'—that modern euphemism for transformation that promises a changed appearance and life circumstances. I researched procedures, followed social media accounts of women with 'perfect' bodies, and convinced myself that physical transformation would heal my inner wounds. My 'glow-up' wasn't fueled by healthy self-care but by corrosive insecurity—by the lie that God had somehow made a mistake when creating me that needed surgical correction.

I couldn't see then how this obsession contradicted everything I had glimpsed during my spiritual journey. In those moments between worlds, I had experienced unconditional acceptance—a love that saw beyond physical appearance to the essence of who I was. Yet here I was, back in my body, rejecting that very body as unworthy, unlovable, and insufficient. The disconnect between my spiritual experience and my physical self-rejection created a fracture through which the enemy could whisper increasingly dangerous suggestions.

I had taken every weight loss pill and worked out 5 to 6 days a week. Nothing worked. I wore my waist trainer until I was blue, yet I was still unsatisfied. Nothing I did made me feel confident in my body.

One day, I was called to the kitchen table where my grandmother sat. Her eyes held wisdom born from decades of watching family patterns repeat. "Shabriya, don't you think you're losing enough weight?" she asked, her voice carrying a tremor I chose not to hear.

This had become our routine—she questioned my rapid weight loss every other day, and I dismissed her concerns with increasing irritation. "No, Mimi. I'm fine. Leave me alone," I responded automatically, the harshness in my tone a defense against her scrutiny.

What happened next should have stopped me in my tracks. My grandmother, strong and stoic, the family cornerstone, began to cry. Not gentle tears of sadness, but the desperate weeping of someone witnessing a tragedy they cannot prevent.

"What now?" I asked, uncomfortable with her display of emotion.

"Oh, Shabriya," she pleaded, "are you on drugs? Please, please stop taking drugs."

I laughed, genuinely amused by what seemed an absurd conclusion. "Are you serious? You're always hyping it," I dismissed, failing to recognize the gift being offered—the gift of perspective from someone who had seen this before.

In hindsight, I wish I had taken her comment more seriously and recognized it for what it was: a divine warning delivered through the vessel of an experienced elder. Scripture reminds us that "the way of a fool is right in his own eyes, but he who heeds counsel is wise" (Proverbs 12:15). My grandmother's tears weren't merely familial concern; they were spiritual discernment that I lacked in my obsession.

Her husband—my grandfather—had battled drug addiction for many years. She recognized in my behavior, rapidly changing appearance, and defensive reactions, the same patterns she had witnessed. She had seen how addiction begins not with substances but with obsession, with the willingness to harm oneself in pursuit of a goal that promises relief but delivers destruction.

What I perceived as her overreaction was prophetic insight. Every time I looked in the mirror, I saw only a "lonely fat girl with acne." I was blind to the beautiful young woman recovering from a life-threatening condition, blind to the miracle of being alive at all. I hated that former version of myself—"the reason I had no friends, the reason I felt ugly, the reason I was abused. Always getting me into dumb situations, never standing up for myself, a single mother with a creepy old baby daddy. She was embarrassing, and I couldn't return to being her."

This self-hatred wasn't just psychological; it was spiritual warfare—the enemy using my insecurities to drive me toward self-destruction. My grandmother sensed this danger, but I was too entranced by the false promise of physical transformation to hear the spiritual warning in her tears.

I decided to move forward with the surgery, my determination hardened by each perceived rejection and fueled by social media images of 'after' bodies that promised happiness. The first surgeon backed out after reviewing my stroke history, even though I had discussed it thoroughly during my consultation and had even obtained clearance from my neurosurgeon about the risks.

"There is a way that appears to be right, but in the end it leads to death." (Proverbs 14:12)

In that moment of rejection, I had a choice: to recognize this as divine intervention—a protective barrier preventing me from potential harm—or to view it as merely an obstacle to overcome in pursuit of my goal. I chose the latter, overlooking a red flag waving vigorously in my path.

The surgeon's refusal wasn't a challenge to overcome but a mercy I refused to accept. Instead of questioning my path, I sought another doorway—evidence of what Scripture calls "a stubborn and rebellious heart" (Jeremiah 5:23).

The surgeon I had been following on social media for years had finally opened his clinic, which seemed like perfect timing—a sign that everything was falling into place rather than falling apart. When I discovered there had been a death at his previous location, the rational part of my brain registered alarm. But his staff quickly assured me it wasn't his fault, it was a different surgeon he worked with, offering explanations that soothed my concerns without addressing them.

Looking back, I can see how the enemy uses our desperation to dull our discernment. Every warning sign was reinterpreted through the lens of my obsession: a surgeon's refusal became an unfair obstacle; a patient's death became an unfortunate coincidence; my grandmother's tears became an emotional overreaction. God placed barricades across my path while I found detours around His protection.

This willful blindness wasn't new to me. Throughout Scripture, God's people repeatedly ignore divine warnings, rushing headlong into danger while convinced they're pursuing blessing. The Israelites had been warned against alliances with foreign nations, yet they repeatedly sought security in these relationships rather than trusting God's protection. Similarly, I was seeking security in physical transformation rather than in the God who had already saved my life once through miraculous intervention.

With each warning sign dismissed, I moved further from divine wisdom and closer to a situation requiring divine rescue while convincing myself I was being persistent in pursuing my desires.

I scheduled my appointment and spent months saving every penny for my surgery. I was all set.

I asked Drew to go, but he refused. He disagreed with my decision, yet I convinced myself, him, and everyone else that this was something I had always wanted and that I was doing it for me. I just wanted to achieve better results because the outcomes I was getting from working out were not giving me the body I desired. It's just a tweak; it's not that serious. I said everything I could to convince myself and my family that I was comfortable and confident in my decision.

I even prayed about it daily and asked God to make sure I made it back to my daughter. At that time, a couple of women had died from undergoing the surgery. I didn't want to scare myself into not getting it or wasting money I couldn't get back. I also had to sit and ask myself if I was comfortable with the idea that I might die and not come back to raise my daughter. The truth is, I wasn't; I was scared. But I allowed myself to believe the lies the clinics and surgeons told me. I clicked on links on their websites, thinking they gave me accurate information about board-certified surgeons, which I later discovered was false. I allowed myself to believe lies about myself, my body, and the necessity of the surgery because of my pride and ego. Even with all these red flags, I was still prepared to go.

After purchasing all the foam boards, fajas, pain relief items, itch cream, scar cream, bandages, massages, etc.,

I had invested so much time, effort, and money that there was no backing out. The day before I was set to leave, Drew told me again, "You know you don't have to do this." "What do you mean?" I replied. "I don't want you doing any of this for me." I heard him, yet I did not believe him. I thought we had both been excited about this for months, or at least he was excited for me. And now, he said not to do it for him the day before. I began to believe his concern was more about who he thought I would become when I was confident than his concern for me. "Everything is already set. You're welcome to come, but you don't have to. Can you drop me off at the airport tomorrow?" I was filled with anxiety and overwhelmed. This was my first time flying, so I thought it was just jitters. I was so wrong.

The moment I landed in Miami, I was annoyed. This was my first time at any airport, so I must have exited through the wrong gate. It was hot, pouring down rain and thundering at the same time. This was my first time leaving California, except for a few road trips to Reno and one disastrous trip to Vegas with my sister and cousins.

The airport was so overcrowded and overwhelming that I became paralyzed with anxiety. The person from the recovery house who was supposed to pick me up was at a different gate—probably the one I should have used. I didn't know how to explain my location, which made her frustrated and annoyed with me. I asked a worker for help, which added another 30 minutes to my time getting to her. With each passing minute, my anxiety grew. The lady didn't seem very friendly or understanding, and I knew I would have to rely on her to drive around and get food in a city I knew nothing about.

We arrived at the recovery house, and they showed me
around. They introduced me to my room and roommate.
They also showed me the kitchen, the bathroom, and explained what the schedule would be like. It was packed, but
nothing spectacular. This home was filled with other wom-
en, the majority, if not all, being Black women, just like
me, excited to have surgery. We were all undergoing BBLs,
with some getting complete mommy makeovers, changing
everything about ourselves, all hoping to come out better
than we came in. I was thrilled to be surrounded by other
women who shared my desires. No one was telling me "No"
or that I shouldn't do it. Everyone was rejoicing and excited
for me and my decision, and I was also excited for them.
I had connected with a community that encouraged and supported my desires, yet I still felt an overwhelming amount
of anxiety and a sense that I didn't belong. I ignored it and
continued with the process. The day before my surgery, I
was dropped off at the surgery clinic for an in-person consultation and to sign paperwork.

I waited 6-8 hours in the waiting room for the doctor to see
me. With each passing hour, my anxiety and desire to leave
grew, and I was constantly reminded of how much nonre-
fundable money I had invested. That kept me there. Finally,
the doctor called me and another young woman to be seen.
I showed him pictures of my desired results and asked if he
wanted anything from my doctor again for the hundredth
time. Again, he assured me it was fine, but the conversation
felt rushed as we were shuffled off to the next office to sign
paperwork. Then, we were hit with an additional bill—an
extra $700 on top of the thousands I had already paid be-
cause they failed to inform us that we would need a specific
type of faja and binder immediately after the surgery. At
this point, I was ready to leave. There were no stores where
I could find the items, and my appointment was set for

tomorrow morning. They offered me the 1st appointment of the day to compensate for the inconvenience of waiting on them all day, which I gladly accepted, believing that at least I wouldn't have to be there all day tomorrow.

The morning arrived, and I was filled with nerves. I had come alone and noticed that most other girls had friends or family. I tried not to let it bother me, but it did. I constantly questioned if I had made a mistake by choosing to come alone. Ignoring my growing hesitation, I decided to continue with the process. I had spoken with the anesthesiologist and underwent a drug and pregnancy test. The assistant came in and told me my test came back positive. POSITIVE FOR WHAT!? I yelled, as if I hadn't already known. Positive for THC. I mumbled to myself that I thought it would be out by now. OK, but they said I couldn't smoke for 20 days, and it's been 20 days. She replied, " I'll tell the anesthesiologist to talk to you. When the anesthesiologist came in, he questioned me about my smoking and then about my medical history and past anesthesia. His face looked shocked Once I explained that I had a stroke, he immediately said, "No, I'm going to need something from your doctor." He felt uncomfortable continuing with the anesthesia without a risk assessment from my neurologist. "Man, I asked the surgeon several times if there was anything he needed from my doctor, and he said no! I spoke to my doctor before I booked; I could've sorted this out before I left." He stood firm on his no. I had to request the assessment, but my doctor's office was three hours behind. I decided to wait in the waiting room until my doctor's office opened in a few hours. Once it opened, I contacted someone immediately, but the doctor wasn't in yet. I explained the situation to them, and the nurse was happy to get the doctor to send something over as soon as he arrived. I waited and

waited and waited some more. Finally, after hours of waiting and being unable to eat, one of the coordinators told me
my doctor had faxed the information. I could have easily
lied about my medical history, but I wanted transparency. I
told myself I didn't want to undergo surgery if my medical
history would make it more dangerous. Honestly, I've read
enough articles about women dying during this surgery to
know that if I concealed this information and something
went wrong, they would use that as an excuse for my death.
As a reason, I "deserved" to die. With all that going on, you
would think I would take these as signs and God's grace,
as reasons not to get this surgery. But something inside
me just wouldn't let it go. I downplayed the risk by telling
myself, "Well, with brain surgery, I had a risk of dying too,
so what's the difference?"

I can answer this question now. The difference between
having a surgery that could save your life and choosing to
risk your life by undergoing a cosmetic enhancement that
you do not need, making a decision to undergo the deadliest
surgery that exists for some booty, is significantly different... I was choosing to risk my life and possibly die, and
risk not being around for my daughter, I was selfish. Consumed by my low Self-worth and ego. I didn't know then
what I know now: that I am beautifully and wonderfully
made, created in His likeness, and that God makes no mistakes. Instead of seeking the Lord and allowing His Holy
Spirit to fill and uplift me, I was chasing things and taking
risks that only made me feel emptier. The stroke wasn't my
fault. But if I had died on the BBL table, it would have very
well been a result of my choices—what I chose to priori-
tize.

When Beauty Nearly Killed

I went back to the clinic and sat there anxiously waiting. The time finally came; I hadn't eaten all day. I was exhausted. I had spent the last 12 hours in this clinic waiting for the surgery, and I was the very last patient when the plan had originally been for me to be the first. It didn't matter; I was here now. As I sat waiting for the doctor to call me, I looked in the mirror at all the markings and imperfections that would be fixed in just a few short hours, thinking about how beautiful I was about to become. I called my grandmother right before I went into the surgery room, filled with an overwhelming urge to pray. She prayed over me, prayed for the doctors that the Lord may guide them, and that I would make it back home safely. As I said amen, I came into agreement with her prayers. Then I was called back; it was finally time. I sat at the table, excited about the change that was coming. The anesthesiologist prepared my mask and said, "OK, Miss Hill, we're finally here!" He told me to start counting down, beginning at 10... 9... 8... 7... 6......
Anxiety started to lift, and sleepiness began to set in.

ZzzZzzZzzzZzz

"Ms. Hill. MS. HILL. Hey. Welcome back! Surgery went great. It's OK; you're still drowsy from the anesthesia."

I felt extremely weak, but it's okay. They said it was just the anesthesia. I will be OK. My eyelids felt like weights. I tried to speak, but nothing came out. I drifted back to sleep while waiting for the anesthesia to wear off. I woke up trying to move, but I couldn't. My whole body was freezing and wet, like I was drenched in ice water. I was trembling uncontrollably. Something is wrong, I thought to myself. Hello... I tried to yell, but I could only manage a faint whisper. A man who was sweeping nearby saw me struggling to get up and called over to a lady in Spanish. The lady was trying to help me up, but my body was too weak. She started frantically running around, speaking to the man in Spanish. I couldn't understand. She brought me a glass and asked me to drink in broken English, saying it would help. "I can't," I whispered. "911. Call, please, hospital." "No, it's okay. Drink, drink milk. It helps." Everything went black as I was falling… falling into darkness. On my way down, I could hear my mom screeching. I listened to my sister's voice screaming, "Noooooooo!" "Shayla!" I yelled back. I could hear my daughter crying, with angry and sad faces. "Shabriyaaaaa!" my grandmother screamed. A father's voice told me to return, "GO BACK!" but I only fell deeper into the darkness. The screams turned into anguish, painful cries of voices I didn't recognize. It was nothing like the peace and light I walked into when I had my stroke. In fact, it was the complete opposite. Shame had overtaken me, freezing me in my fall.

Once again, I found myself in a situation begging God to spare my life. this time, I felt undeserving due to the choices I had willingly made. Lord, please, I'm sorry that I even did this. I repent, Lord God, please allow me to go back home. I'm sorry; I want to go back home. Yet if it is your will, Lord, let it be done. I felt my back hit the cold, wet sheets. It was my blood. I opened my eyes again to see the cleaning man and nurse, hovering over me. The nurse was still trying to give me milk when I realized my surgeon, my doctor, had left without even ensuring that I was okay. "Policia, policia," I whispered, trying to remember any emergency words I learned in my high school Spanish class—still, nothing—just milk and an attempt to force me off the gurney. I could hear my phone repeatedly, vibrating and ringing in the distance, ding ding ding.

Everyone must be worried. I tried to ask for my phone, but again, no words came. Wow, God, so this is how it ends? I'm going to die in the back of a BBL clinic with two people who don't even speak English and won't even call me an ambulance. I'm going to bleed out on this damn gurney all because of my stubbornness my selfish pride... I'm sorry. Forgive me. I continued mentally preparing myself for the inevitable. I was going to die here. I prayed crying softly. Tears rolling down my face, Lord, thank you for trying to save and warn me.

I was so obsessed; I refused to see the signs. Lord I'm sorry I wasted my second chance at life. I repent for my sins, and I understand If you don't forgive me. But please Lord, will you protect my daughter? Comfort my mother and family. I'm so sorry I did this to them. Lord, stay with me in this moment. I accepted my fate and was at peace. I knew I was undeserving of a miracle; I just didn't want to die alone. I wanted to feel his presence through my transition. Suddenly I had a thought, one that seemed out of place, separate from my own. Don't forget your promise. Suddenly I remembered my promise to make it back home. Lord, I made a promise, and I know you will make sure I make it home. You did it before, and you can do it again. Nothing is too big or too small for you.

As I lay there, drifting in and out of consciousness, my blood soaking through the surgical sheets, I heard an ambulance siren—faint at first, then growing louder. In my semiconscious state, the sound seemed disconnected from my situation, a background noise in someone else's emergency. I didn't realize then that they were coming for me, that my life hung in a precarious balance between negligence and rescue.

> *"For he will command his angels concerning you to guard you in all your ways." (Psalm 91:11)*

Through blurred vision, I watched as emergency personnel rushed into the room, their voices sharp with urgency, their movements precise. They transferred me onto their gurney with practiced efficiency, my body limp and unresisting. As they rushed me toward the ambulance, I could hear screaming, desperate, angry shouting that cut through my mental fog.

I would later learn this was the recovery house owner, a woman I had never met but had become my unlikely advocate. She had been waiting outside the clinic for hours, growing increasingly concerned by the surgeon's evasive explanations about my extended recovery. When her instincts told her something was wrong, she had threatened to call the police if they didn't produce me immediately. Her intervention—the advocacy of a stranger—became the human instrument of divine rescue.

When I opened my eyes inside the ambulance, something extraordinary happened. The emergency medical technicians working frantically to stabilize me appeared transformed—their faces seemed to glow with an otherworldly light, their movements synchronized with supernatural purpose. In my semiconscious state, I recognized them not merely as medical professionals but as angels—divine messengers sent to snatch me from death's threshold.

This wasn't metaphorical language or poetic interpretation. The veil between physical and spiritual realms again thinned in that moment, allowing me to perceive the divine presence operating through human hands. Scripture tells us that God "will command his angels concerning you to guard you in all your ways" (Psalm 91:11), and in that ambulance, I experienced the literal truth of this promise.

Despite the physical crisis—my body in shock, my blood pressure dangerously low, my systems beginning to fail—I felt a profound peace wash over me. This peace wasn't denial or delusion; it was recognition. The same divine presence that had met me during my stroke, that had walked with me through heavenly gardens when my body lay unconscious, was present now in this Miami ambulance. God's faithfulness hadn't faltered, even when my wisdom had.

As I surrendered to unconsciousness again, I carried this certainty with me into the darkness: the God who had brought me back once would do so again. Not because I deserved it—my foolish choices had placed me in this danger—but because His mercy transcends our mistakes. I went to sleep not in fear but in trust, even as my physical body fought for survival.

The next time I opened my eyes, I was in the hospital, and a team of doctors was working on me. I looked at one of the nurses, opened my mouth, and this time, words came out.
"Am I going to be okay?"
... "I don't know," he said quietly, with a genuinely concerned look.
"Please call my mom..." I felt weak again.
I began to pray until I lost consciousness.
I opened my eyes. "Mom?!"
I wasn't sure if it was real or how much time had passed.

"MOM?"
"Yes," she said, rushing toward me. Her face was filled with stress and worry.
"I'm sorry."

Little did I know, my mom had already been on a flight to Miami when she heard the news. My entire family received news that I had died on the table. (To this day, it's still unclear how), Though it was almost true. My surgeon left me to die on the table with a janitor and an assistant of some sort. (I believe a nurse would have taken the situation more seriously, but maybe not.) I woke up the next day feeling better and more energized, with my phone ringing off the hook—calls, texts, voicemails—the news had already picked up the story and requested interviews as if I wasn't just fighting for my life. They were even contacting my mom. My mom, relieved to see me up and talking, began to explain the severity of the situation. The night before, as she sat in the waiting room in tears, praying for my recovery, she had met another mother doing the same. They started conversing and realized their daughters were going through the same ordeal. Her daughter had also had BBL surgery, and she was rushed to the hospital from their hotel. Her symptoms were surprisingly identical to mine. As they talked and shared a 'what a coincidence' moment, another woman (a third woman) was rushed into the emergency room, who also had a BBL that day.

(Now, anyone with experience being lectured by a black mom after making a not-so-smart decision knows what happened next. Once she realized that I wasn't going to die, she went on and on about how it wasn't just me, but also two other women she had just seen. How we all ignorantly paid these idiots to put us in danger. How I wasted all this money to fly out here for this Insert expletive here to kill me. She had to fly alllll the way to Miami, thinking I was dead. Now that the threat had subsided, her lecturing was nonstop, and to this day, she will not hesitate to remind me how she "had to fly across the country" if she thinks I'm taking any huge risks.) "Tap tap. There was a light knock on the door. "Come in" welcoming anything that would give me a break from my mom's lecturing. "Hi, I just wanted to check on your mom"— Gasp! She looked at me in shock and horror.

"You were at the clinic!? " She shouted in surprise.

"Oh yeah, I was talking to you while I was waiting." I responded.

"How's your daughter? Wait, IS SHE IN HERE TOO? ARE YOU SERIOUS?!" I asked, shocked and confused that we were at the same clinic and now in the same Hospital ICU.

"Yes, I told them something was wrong in the recovery area, but they still just said it was normal and sent us home. I brought her here afterwards." The woman my mother had met in the waiting area came to check on her. It wasn't until that moment that we realized it wasn't just me who had nearly died due to this one surgeon. A couple of days later, we found out there were three of us, in the same hospital ICU and we had all undergone BBL surgery that day at the same clinic with the same "surgeon". The clinic was able to discredit the third woman because she lied about her medical history, even though her medical history wasn't the reason the 3 of us were in the hospital with severe staph infections. I received 11 blood transfusions, just for my body to come out of the shock and distress it was under. My blood-soaked faja and binder, which they wrapped tightly around my waist, were the only things that kept me from bleeding out entirely before reaching the hospital. The outcome would have been deadly if they had waited any longer. The media had been contacting them as well. Our moms were angry, rightfully so. They wanted to expose what this surgery and this "surgeon" had done to us. I wanted to hide. I started feeling ashamed and selfish about my decision, but I understood the importance of sharing what happened. I wanted to show women, especially those who look like me, who were dying because of the surgery, what could happen. So, I agreed to give a statement and sent photos to be used. Chaos ensued...

The hospital called in a real plastic surgeon who checked my surgical incisions and drainage related to the BBL and introduced himself as a United States board-certified plastic surgeon licensed in Florida and California. I thought it was odd, but I ignored it and introduced myself anyway. "It's Shabriya. It's nice to meet you. " He asked if my surgeon had come in to check on me. "No," I replied. "Has he at least called?" he asked, seemingly annoyed. Nope. He was shocked ... and explained that he would take over my care. "A real plastic surgeon would be needed to care for you in the hospital." The comment made me feel uneasy. "What do you mean by a real plastic surgeon?" "I mean a United States board-certified plastic surgeon." I was confused; I didn't understand. "Was my doctor not certified?" "Not by the U.S. board of plastics." He said very matter-of-fact. "But they have a link to his certifications on the website." It's not the same. I was still confused, but I moved on anyway. "So, when will I get to go home?"

"It depends on your recovery. But you cannot leave until your drain is removed. Let's see how you recover, and I'll check in tomorrow and be back the next day."

"Okay." That sounds good. I didn't know what to make of his comments; he seemed terribly upset. I was just glad he was here to help. By that evening, my face was all over the news in Miami. By morning, my face and Mom's interview were on news stations throughout America and the internet. I felt like this was my opportunity to share my testimony—until I read the comments...

The comments were some of the most disrespectful, ignorant things I have ever read. I didn't even know these people, yet they were judging me and tearing me down, saying how I should have died, how I hated myself, and making excuses for the clinic and doctor. It was discouraging. It got so bad that my sister and cousins argued in the comments, trying to confront those people for how badly they spoke about me. I asked them to stop engaging with people we did not know. They would never talk to me like that in person. I didn't want them wasting time on foolishness. After reading the comments, I was overcome with guilt and shame. I felt a heaviness of shame come and sit-down right on top of me.

I refused to take any more interviews and canceled the ones I had already scheduled. The other woman, continued to take interviews and discuss what happened, but I just wanted it to be over. I spent my time focusing on my recovery. The clinic (Dr. McDonalds's assistant) reached out days later. I was furious and didn't feel like having a superficial conversation. She asked me to come in for a follow-up. "How? I'm in the hospital! " I snapped. I almost died! It was as if they didn't even care, trying to act like they didn't know—as if I weren't rushed away from their clinic by an ambulance. The owner of the recovery house also came to visit and helped me change and clean my blood-soaked garments. She began to tell me what she experienced that night as I lay in the back of that clinic. She told me that she waited outside the exit for hours during and after my surgery, calling my phone, calling the clinic, and even banging on the door for answers. The same woman who could only offer me milk in broken English made every excuse she could, telling lies about how the surgery ran long and that I was still coming off anesthesia, when in reality, I was desperately clinging to my last moments of life. She started to get suspicious and worried when she demanded to see me, at least to ensure I was okay. But the assistant flat-out refused and would not allow her in. She had been doing this for years, even undergoing the surgery herself; she knew this was not the norm. Fearing the worst, she contacted my emergency contact (my mom). And she threatened to call the police if they did not produce her client; the threat of police intervention was enough for them to call for help. Just thinking about the disregard for my life is terrifying. The way the clinic prioritized its reputation and name over human life is a red flag and an unfortunate regular practice in Florida, as cosmetic enhancements lack standard regulation and enforcement. Who knows how many more times they have treated women like this? I was discharged after nearly two weeks, yet it was still unsafe to fly back home. We stayed in hotels while meeting with the plastic surgeon, who continued to express disdain for the entire situation. He even called the doctor and vented his anger at him for having three patients in the hospital whom he had nearly killed. He hadn't even checked on any of them, not even one, to ensure they were alive. He was distraught, tasked with cleaning up the mess left behind from a self proclaimed surgeon. And unfortunately, this wasn't the first time. I only received a follow-up call from Dr. McDonald about a week later. There was no empathy, maybe a generic apology if any at all. I ended the conversation knowing that we would never speak again.

The comment about the US board certification weighed heavily on my mind. So, I asked my real surgeon about it; I even pulled up the website and the link they provided to check the doctors' certifications. He pulled out his business card and said, "This is the actual website." The difference was merely a few letters and a hyphen, which is too subtle to notice when you don't know what to look for. It felt like they had intentionally set up the site to deceive potential customers. He went on to explain how Miami has effectively created death traps. That the Brazilian Butt Lift (BBL) is the most dangerous surgery one can undergo, with the highest death rate. In Florida, one does not need to attend school and complete the necessary hours to become a plastic surgeon; one only needs to be an MD. This means that dentists, ophthalmologists, or orthopedic doctors (like my surgeon) could pursue any MD that requires the least number of hours and education to establish any cosmetic practice in Florida.

They would work on 15+ patients a day (which I learned is way too much for any surgeon), then when they kill someone or have a scandal like what occurred, they would work to discredit the patient whilst shutting down and reopening with a new name a few weeks or months later once things died down. And they did this over and over again. It allowed them not to take responsibility or accountability for what they have done, botch and kill women, and keep going, all for cash. As you can imagine, it's a very deadly, lucrative business in Florida.

Chapter 7
The Battlefield

Fighting for a Soul

"And we know that in all things God works for the good of those who love him, who have been called according to his purpose."- (Romans 8:28)

"Wow," I whispered as the full weight of what I had learned settled upon me. I felt foolish—not just temporarily embarrassed but profoundly awakened to how thoroughly I had been deceived. I had willingly entered a system designed to profit from insecurity, a predatory industry that had found in wounded Black women a particularly vulnerable market. My obsession with physical transformation had overridden my physical and spiritual intuition, nearly costing me my life.

I was overwhelmed with gratitude to God for His intervention—not just in the miraculous eleventh-hour rescue through the ambulance, but in the divine orchestration that had placed the recovery house owner in my path, that had sustained me through multiple blood transfusions, that had brought a legitimate surgeon to take over my care when the impostor who had endangered me abandoned his responsibility.

Walking out of the hospital for the third time in my young life—each exit representing another round of divine mercy—I appeared remarkably unscathed. Looking at me, no one would guess the nearness of my encounter with death, the severity of the medical crisis I had endured. "All praise to Jesus," I whispered, recognizing that my external appearance of wellness was a miracle, another manifestation of God's grace.

In that moment of gratitude, a covenant formed within my heart: "I promised myself that I would never do anything like that again." This wasn't merely a pragmatic decision based on danger assessment; it was a spiritual awakening to the truth that Scripture had been proclaiming all along: that I was "fearfully and wonderfully made" (Psalm 139:14), that "the Lord does not look at the things people look at. People look at the outward appearance, but the Lord looks at the heart" (1 Samuel 16:7).

The statistics I had casually dismissed before surgery now took on faces and names: Black and brown women were dying for BBLs, and I had nearly become another anonymous data point in that tragic tally. What had seemed worth dying for before surgery now appeared as the hollow promise it had always been—a deception explicitly marketed to women like me, who had been conditioned to see their natural bodies as inherently deficient.

This realization transcended mere regret over a dangerous decision. It represented a fundamental shift in how I understood my value and purpose. The God who had created me, who had twice intervened to preserve my life, had not made a mistake in my design. The flaws I perceived were not in my body but in the cultural and spiritual lenses through which I had been taught to view myself.

As I prepared to leave Miami, I carried with me not just the physical scars of this experience but a spiritual conviction that would become increasingly central to my identity: God does not create junk. My worth was never dependent on conforming to manufactured beauty standards. The body I had been so desperate to change had been fearfully and wonderfully made by a Creator who does not err in His craftsmanship.

I came home to a boyfriend who looked at me differently. I'm sure he didn't understand why I felt the need to have this surgery when he loved me for who I am. He didn't realize that I did not feel loved or desired by him. I never told him about all the lies I caught him in because I didn't see the point, knowing I would only end up hurt and I probably wouldn't leave. I ignored his lies, aware he wouldn't change, but I could.

"Love is patient, love is kind. It does not envy, it does not boast, it is not proud. It does not dishonor others, it is not self-seeking, it is not easily angered, it keeps no record of wrongs." (1 Corinthians 13:4-5)

He cared for me throughout my recovery while attempting to sabotage my results along the way. He would sneaki-ly push and smooth down the areas he thought were too large. Making me more self-conscious than ever before. By summer I was done healing. In search of an escape from my reality, I planned a bunch of various trips throughout the summer. 1st up was a girl's trip with my family.

Alcohol, sex, and parties had become an everyday occur-rence, as I tried to escape my shame and embarrassment. My sister, all my girl cousins, and I had been planning a trip to Cancun for Memorial Day. We had been prepar-ing for nearly a year. It would be my first time out of the U.S., and it was guaranteed to be "lit"—or at least that's what they told me. I invited Drew; I wanted him to come; we had barely separated since I came home from Miami, and he gave me a false sense of security and protection, I was afraid to leave behind. I prepared for weeks, trying on clothes to get his opinion. I didn't want him to feel disrespected or uncomfortable in any way. It was time to leave, and he drove me to the airport. On the way, he informed me he would have someone in Cancun check in on me and that I could go with in case of an emergency. I was ok with that.

As soon as we landed, I loved it. The weather was lovely, the ocean was stunning, there were many gorgeous people, and the drinks flowed. I felt welcomed with open arms— something unexpected in this foreign place, yet comforting simultaneously.

The first two nights were overwhelming. My new build had brought me a ton of unwanted attention when I was more comfortable fading into the background. I spent a lot of time texting Drew, sending him pictures, and talking with him. We had spent every day together since we started our relationship, and I missed him, and I honestly just wanted to go home. I called him repeatedly on the third day but could not reach him. Many hours later, when he finally answered, I had already considered breaking up.

"You look like you're having a good time," he answered.
"What?" I asked confused
"My friend saw you getting on the elevator with some guy."
"What guy?" I scanned my thoughts for what he could be talking about.
"Oh, him? That's my cousin's friend, remember? I told you my cousins are friends with a group of guys they also dated, and my cousins were drifting through the group. I've met them several times before, and we've hung out and partied in group settings. We're just cordial, he's friends with my cousins. He was with my cousin, so it wasn't anything

like that; we just got on the same elevator and were talking because we knew each other." I tried to explain an innocent situation, but it was too late. Something shifted. I knew he didn't believe me, even though it was the truth. "I think it's strange… your friend, spying on me; he hasn't even said hello."

"No, he's not; I think he's got some friends staying in your hotel."

"Oh, okay."

"Yeah, have fun."

"I love yo"— Did he hang up on me?!

"Shabriya!" my cousins interrupted, annoyed by how much I constantly wandered off to sneak moments with Drew.

But this vacation, I spent so much time planning seemed to be taking a toll on my relationship, but I trusted him and thought he trusted me.

The next day, we conversed with a group of my cousins guy friends about whether we can trust our partners while away. The men seemed to firmly believe that while we're gone, our boyfriends must be cheating, and that we might as well not worry about being faithful to them because they're not loyal to us while we're away. They argued that if they weren't worried about us going on that trip, then they're cheating. The claim was that, "that's just what men do." "Yes, he can love you. He might genuinely love you, but you're away. He's going to cheat."

So why should you be faithful? The idea seemed ridiculous, to me.

We went back and forth for a while, and I firmly believed what the women were saying. However, my argument was more about convincing myself than them, especially since

Drew had gone silent again. I asked my cousin to speak to her boyfriend and see if he was with Drew, given they had become friends. He wasn't. He finally responded to my call late that night. "Hey, is everything alright?"

"Yes."

"What are you doing? Why didn't you answer my calls?"

"I was hanging out."

"Well, with who? Why would that stop you from answering my calls?"

"I ran into a friend at the store. She was having something at her house and invited me."

"Ok…" So, you went?

Yeah.

Everything from that conversation came rushing back to my mind like crashing waves. My eyes began to strain and tighten.

"Oh, ok. What friend?"

"Someone from school. "

"What school? Is it anyone I know? "

"Nah, you don't know her."

"OK, please help me understand. So, you seen someone at the store, went to her house, and stopped answering my calls? You didn't want to tell me? "

"I didn't know I had to. "

"OK". A tear slipped down my cheek, my chest tightened, and my throat was dry. I had no idea what to say. I was too afraid just to come out and say it. My heart would be too broken if the answer were yes.

And I was stuck in Mexico for 3 more days.

"Well, were you using my car? "

"That's what you care about." He fired back, angry that my line of question came off as if I didn't care. He did not realize that every word that left my lips had been perfectly crafted and rehearsed in my mind as a form of protection from a harsh truth I wasn't ready to hear.

"Hmm, I trust you. " I quickly convinced myself that this had to be a joke. He had to be lying just to try to get under my skin. "Can you just be honest with me!? If you have a problem with me being out here or talking to men I know, why wouldn't you say that? Why act as if you didn't care? As if it's not a big deal? You even encouraged me to go. " "It's not that I don't trust you." "Then why would you do that just to be petty!? I was telling the truth. I've already informed you about these people." "Ok, Shabriya. Ok."

My relationship was probably over, and I was eager to ease the pain of our conversation. I ran to what I believed was my comforter. I sought comfort in weed and alcohol, my desire to feel loved and valued once again making me an easy, vulnerable target to an influx of men who lusted after my body in ways I had not experienced before. I knew they didn't care about me, only how my body could potentially make them feel... I couldn't sleep, so I decided to leave my hotel room and entered the packed bar alone, and sat down and started ordering drinks seeking the solace I knew liquor would provide, even if only temporarily. I was halfway through my second watered-down drink, in deep thought about my failing relationship. When one of the guys I had briefly chatted with came over to talk. I wasn't interested, we barely talked by the pool while his friends were flirting with my cousins. Here I was again engaging in small talk because I didn't want to be rude. Eventually, I excused myself. "Well, it was nice talking to you. I'm going to call it a night." "Why? the party is still going! I like talking to you. Have one more drink with me," he responded in a friendly tone. "No, I really should go." "It won't hurt to have a drink. Come on, enjoy one last drink before you go," he persisted, holding my arm. Preventing me from leaving. I was uncomfortable but I agreed. "Okay, sure, one drink won't hurt." I watched carefully as the bartender made my drink. He picked it up and handed it to me, I didn't close my eyes or turn my back. Nothing seemed out of the ordinary.

"Cheers." I took a few sips. My head began to hurt, so I excused myself, " I really should go. Good night. " I was waiting for the elevator, which seemed to take forever. My condition worsened with each passing minute. My head started to spin, and my vision began to blur just as I was about to pass out. Confused, I tried to catch myself because I was perfectly fine moments ago. "Whoa, I got you," I heard a familiar voice. It was the guy from the bar, though I could barely make out his face. His voice seemed... genuinely concerned. "Are you ok? Let me help you to your room." What's your floor? I could barely talk. I tried, but I don't know what happened, my words were slurred. I can't be this drunk, that fast. My eyelids were so heavy I could barely open them. I was rushed off the elevator. I tried to pull away, but my body refused to respond, going limp as my legs buckled under me. It all seemed too familiar, though my memory loss had previously prevented me from understanding why. Not this, not again...

The War Between Truth and Lies

"Cursed are those who put their trust in mere humans, who rely on human strength, and turn their hearts away from the LORD." - Jeremiah 17:5

I had continued to witness God's grace firsthand and be a receiver of his many miracles, yet I lacked the proper guidance to turn my heart fully towards him. I ignored warnings from the Holy Spirit, brushing them off as if they were my confused imagination. I had set myself on a path destined to repeat the same patterns and curses. Yet God remained the same. He never abandoned me, even though I unknowingly continued to abandon him.

The relationship with the man I once thought would be my husband had to end—a truth that God had been quietly revealing to me for months before I found the courage to acknowledge it.

"Do not be yoked together with unbelievers. For what do righteousness and wickedness have in common? Or what fellowship can light have with darkness?" (2 Corinthians 6:14)

I had clung desperately to the crumbs of love he offered, mistaking them for sustenance, convincing myself that partial affection was better than complete solitude. Scripture says that "love is patient, love is kind... it is not self-seeking, it is not easily angered" (1 Corinthians 13:45), yet our relationship consistently failed to reflect these divine attributes. Still, I remained, trapped in a spiritual compromise that muted my connection with God even as I pretended otherwise.

When I returned home from Cancun, I had night terrors about the man I met at the bar. I couldn't piece together what happened, but somehow Drew was able to fill in the blanks. Knowing all the details, he said he learned from a "friend".
In my shock and horror, I ran to my Dr. and explained the situation. She was confused, questioning me on how my boyfriend knew all this information if he wasn't there.
"His friend was there, and he told him. I guess"
"Shabriya that doesn't make any sense."

"I know but I don't know what's going on"
"It sounds like you were drugged"
"How?" I was careful or so I thought.
Confused by her statement and now looking at her face
she was visibly concerned. She questioned my relationship
asking if I was "sure my about my boyfriend" I was, or at
least I thought so, until she asked that question.
I became unsure of my relationship, "Even my Dr. realized
the red flags in my relationship with the limited information I gave. Her question replayed in my mind repeatedly,
yet I was still unwilling to end it.

Our latest trip together became God's megaphone when
subtler messages had gone unheeded. As Drew became
increasingly drunk and high, his true character emerged
unfiltered, culminating in a baseless accusation that I had
stolen his wallet. I couldn't shake the memory of his transformation: the gentle eyes I trusted hardening with suspi-
cion, his towering frame seeming to grow with rage, his
voice cutting through me with accusations that revealed
how little he truly knew me. In that moment, the scales
fell from my eyes, and I saw clearly what I had refused to
acknowledge for so long.

This revelation wasn't merely personal disappointment; it
was divine intervention. God often uses our painful experiences to reveal truths we've been avoiding. As Proverbs
20:30 tells us, "Blows and wounds scrub away evil, and
beatings purge the inmost being." The emotional wounds
from that confrontation were scrubbing away the illusion
I had constructed about our relationship, purging me of a
connection that had become an idol competing with my
devotion to God.

Each time I replayed the incident in my mind, I wasn't just dwelling on hurt—I was being invited to see clearly, to recognize that God desired more for me than what I had settled for. The man whose anger and violence had become so unpredictable was showing me who he truly was; God was asking me to believe that revelation rather than clinging to who I wished him to be.

After what seemed like a fun day lounging at the pool, we went to our hotel room only to find he had misplaced his wallet.

"Have you seen my wallet?" he asked seriously.

The mood had shifted, but I was too drunk to notice the accusation that came with his question.

"Yeah, you had put it in your pocket at the pool," I slurred.

"It's not there. I checked. Where is my wallet? You were the only one around me."

My innocence closed my eyes to the fact that he was accusing me.

As he angrily checked his luggage and then mine, it became clear.

"Wait, you think I took it? But I'm the one who kept telling you to put it in your pocket so you wouldn't lose it."

He paused from searching my things only to continue drinking from his Hennessy bottle.

"Why would you throw all of my stuff around? Why would I need to steal from you? Be for real..."

We argued back and forth, which ended with him pushing me so hard that I went flying onto the bed. Suddenly, the man I trusted became just another man I feared. I sat there, silent as he continued yelling, only getting up to pick up the pieces from the glass he threw to the floor on his way out, slamming the door behind him.

I had never seen him that angry. Watching his 6'4 ", almost 300-pound frame grow with anger terrified me. Once again, I froze like that scared little girl on the bathroom floor.

I picked up my clothes and folded them. Tears started to soak my clothes as I put them back into my bags. "Wow, all this over a wallet I watched him put away." I went over to his pants and searched the pockets. I didn't find anything. Maybe it fell out on our way up, but we would have heard it.

I checked again, and it was pushed deep down in a secret pocket so he wouldn't lose it. "Great," I thought as I lay down and cried myself to sleep.

I was awakened by someone struggling to get in the door.

"Where was my wallet?" he asked as he picked it up from the dresser.

"It was in your pocket...Like I said."

"We are going to get dinner. Do you want to come?"

I couldn't sit with his family and pretend I didn't hate him.

"No, I just want to rest before I leave. It's only a 3-hour drive."

But I was in no position to drive. I took my bags and head-ed to my car, sleeping it off in the parking lot instead of in a king-size bed with him. I couldn't stand to even look at him.

The violent way he responded confirmed what had been sitting on my heart for months. This relationship was over. He is not the man for me. God surely did not send me such an abusive addict for a husband.

Weeks passed before I got the courage to tell him. I tried to tell him how scared and hurt I was from what happened, but he kept brushing it off as if his drunken state excused the very real fear that continued to linger.

He was a person with a substance use disorder who was unwilling to get help, and I was following closely behind. I had never drunk so much in my life. I never tried drugs in my life before him. I had not gotten in a fight since I was a kid, yet now I was fighting every week, constantly being attacked and jumped by random women I had never even met. I wasn't getting hurt, so I didn't think it was a big deal, but this wasn't me. My mom tried to warn me, but I wouldn't listen until it was too late. The relationship changed me in so many ways, to the point that I no longer recognized myself.

Upon my telling him we should take a break; his drinking was making me very uncomfortable he decided to have sex with a family friend while we were supposed to be figuring things out. The news came from my mom, and immediately, my heart and my world shattered. I couldn't understand why he would want to hurt me like this. I became violent and inconsolable. For months I would black out and find my self circling around the neighborhoods I knew I might find them. Something inside me broke, and rage stepped in and took its place.

Betrayed and deeply depressed, I needed to shift my focus to something productive. I had turned to cooking, hoping it would bring me the same sense of peace and calm as before. After much encouragement from friends and family, I started selling the meals from home. It quickly grew into working out of a commercial kitchen and owning my food trailer. I couldn't believe the doors that were opening. I took all the pain and anger I was experiencing and used it as fuel to start my business.

It's not the heroic story you would think it is. Where do you think the pain and trauma go when we try and fail to bury it? The pain came back! Psalm 55:22 tells us to "Cast your burden on the Lord, and he will sustain you" yet here I was, putting my burdens in an imaginary box and pushing them so deep down that I convinced myself I would never have to deal with them again. I would very soon find out just how wrong I was.

Since I never healed from all that I went through, I had to push it down just to keep moving forward. My body hit a standstill as it refused to continue down the path I was on. My body clinging to the unhealed trauma, recalling all the memories that my "broken" brain desperately tried to protect me from, Night terrors, sleep paralysis, and thoughts questioning if this life was even worth living threatened to end it all. Pure exhaustion had gotten the best of me, my mental health falling to the wayside, unintentionally taking a huge hit. Yet I refused to stop.

As I lay in my bed, exhausted, overworked, and sleep deprived, I was too tired to jump up from my bed as

I usually would, to move away from the window as I heard gunshots ring out. In my exhaustion I felt an overwhelming urge to pray, I fought my sleep just long enough to quickly pray for God to cover anyone in the area and spare the innocent.

As I slowly drifted off to sleep to the sound of tires screeching, screams, and police sirens. I thought it was just "another day in the city."

After three days of work without sleep, I slept the entire day and into the next. I woke up to several missed calls.

"Hey Madre! Wassup?"

"Shabriya, what have you been doing!?"

"Man, I was tired. I've been sleeping."

"They shot up Shayla's car! You didn't hear them shooting?"

My world stopped as I realized that my quick, restless prayer that almost did not happen wasn't for some random stranger but for my sister. I was too tired to check in on her or my nephew, who lived just a few blocks away. Guilt and shame began to creep in.

"What!? WHO?! Is She Ok!?"

My mind flooded with questions, moving quicker than my mouth could process.

What about my nephew!?

"He wasn't there, thank God. Shayla is safe, but she is not ok, her friend didn't make it. She's not taking any calls, but you can try."

I called a few times with no answer before texting. I didn't want to seem selfish or inconsiderate when I reached out to my sister. I felt weird thanking God for one life while another was tragically lost, but I was grateful that she was alive.

"Sorry for your loss. My sincerest condolences." "Thank you," I got a response.

"I thank God you're ok."

I knew it might not be what she wanted to hear, but it needed to be said. I kept thinking back to that moment lying in my bed, the moment I noticed that there were too many shots (more than "normal") and how it sounded like multiple guns. How out of frustration I screamed, "Alright y'all doing too much!" and whispered, "Wow, they want somebody dead."

Now, realizing that it was my sister the whole time, afraid and fleeing to safety.

Weeks later, when she shared that she was left to clean her car herself (I would think the police or somebody else would do that), there was a bullet that was stopped by one of the metal posts in the headrest. A single skinny metal post had seemingly saved her life.

"That's nothing but the Lord!" I shouted, knowing that ONLY God can be that perfect. "The timing, speed, location, and accuracy, necessary for that bullet to hit a thin metal post, stop, and not touch you!"

"Rejoice," I could tell she didn't want to hear all that at that moment, but I was in awe. No one knew I had made a habit out of praying for victims, bystanders, families, and my car that was still sporting the bullet holes from one of the last shootings, after constantly feeling helpless and emotionally wrecked from hearing people die right outside my window. So, all I could do was rejoice, I knew the Lord was with her. I knew that prayer worked!

"Our dad is protecting you!" I excitedly proclaimed; my spiritual understanding still dangerously muddled. In my confused theology, I prayed to both God and my ancestors as if they were interchangeable powers, different faces of the same spiritual reality. I had unwittingly fallen into one of the oldest spiritual traps—idolatry clothed in the respectable garments of cultural tradition and familial reverence.

Ancestral Worship and Divine Jealousy

"For there is one God and one mediator between God and mankind, the man Christ Jesus." (1 Timothy 2:5)

By this point, I had become obsessed with ancestral worship, devoting far more time, energy, and reverence to these practices than I ever gave to God. I built elaborate altars, left meaningful trinkets and gifts, burned sage to "cleanse" spaces, and even cooked my deceased relatives' favorite foods as offerings. These rituals brought a sense of connection and comfort that felt spiritual but lacked divine endorsement.

What I could not see, in my spiritual blindness, was how directly these practices contradicted Scripture. The first commandment explicitly states, "You shall have no other gods before me" (Exodus 20:3), and Deuteronomy 18:1112 specifically warns against consulting the dead. Yet there I was, directing prayers and worship to those who had gone before me rather than to the God who had miraculously preserved my life.

This wasn't an innocent cultural practice but actual spiritual infidelity. I was committing what Scripture calls "spiritual adultery"—giving to created beings the devotion that belongs exclusively to the Creator. The comfort and seemingly positive feelings these rituals produced weren't confirmation of their legitimacy but part of their danger. As Paul warns in 2 Corinthians 11:14, "Satan himself masquerades as an angel of light," making spiritual deception palatable and even temporarily satisfying.

My spiritual confusion wasn't unique or novel; it represented the same pattern of deception that has diverted God's people throughout history. Just as the Israelites repeatedly turned to Baal and Asherah while still claiming to worship Yahweh, I had created a syncretic spiritual practice that allowed me to feel spiritual without the demands of true discipleship. My ancestral worship wasn't complementing my relationship with God; it was competing with it, drawing my heart away from the exclusive devotion He requires and deserves.

My cousin had become infatuated with a local fortune-teller, gradually wearing down my initial skepticism with persistent testimony about transformative readings and spiritual insights. Eventually, I relented—a seemingly minor decision that would open doorways I was spiritually unprepared to navigate.

"Let no one be found among you who... practices divination or sorcery, interprets omens, engages in witchcraft, or casts spells, or who is a medium or spiritist or who consults the dead." (Deuteronomy 18:10-11)

My meeting with the woman who called herself by various spiritually impressive titles—"Priestess," "spiritual advisor," "tarot reader"—marked a dangerous turning point in my spiritual journey. These carefully chosen labels masked the biblical reality of what she was: a practitioner of divination, what Scripture calls a "witch." The warm, incense-scented room with its crystals and candles created a spiritual atmosphere that lacked the hallmarks of actual divine presence.

During our session, she demonstrated knowledge about my life that she could not have known naturally. She spoke of my dad with specific details, described my stroke with uncanny accuracy, and referenced conversations I'd had in private. She claimed to be communicating with a spirit that provided these insights—a spirit I assumed must be the Holy Spirit because of the truthfulness of the information and because she occasionally referenced Scripture or mentioned God.

"Thank you, spirit," she would repeat after each revelation, her deliberate vagueness about which spirit she was addressing serving as spiritual camouflage. She never explicitly claimed this was the Holy Spirit, yet allowed me to make that assumption through calculated ambiguity— something the genuine Holy Spirit later helped me recognize as a red flag. Scripture warns that "even the demons believe—and tremble" (James 2:19), reminding us that spiritual entities can possess factual knowledge without having godly character or purpose.

Her most dangerous deception came packaged as an affirmation: "Girl, spirit has been trying to get your attention for a long time! Do you know how much money you could make talking to these spirits?!" In this framing, the disturbing supernatural experiences I'd been having since my stroke—experiences I had wisely avoided engaging with—were reinterpreted as potential spiritual gifts rather than dangerous temptations. The encounters I had recognized as demonic were cleverly rebranded as ancestral communications, spiritual enlightenment, and even financial opportunity.

The spiritual danger at that moment was profound yet virtually invisible to me. The enemy's most effective deceptions appear not as obvious evil but as reasonable alternatives, spiritual shortcuts, or empowering opportunities. This woman wasn't just reading cards; she was deliberately attempting to redirect my awakening spiritual sensitivity toward demonic resources rather than divine relationship. As Scripture warns, "The Spirit clearly says that in later times some will abandon the faith and follow deceiving spirits and things taught by demons" (1 Timothy 4:1).

And in my ignorance, I believed what she was saying was true. I was "too busy" to study my Bible. I lacked the wisdom to know that just because I prayed to God, "flatten my tires, allow my car to break down. Lord make sure I don't make it to this place if it's not good, if it is not of you Lord protect me from it," the fact that I made it there safely was not a "sign" or the green light to proceed.

And now here I was, passing on my sins and wickedness across my family, adding to the chains and curses that had already followed from generation to generation. (Let me just be honest and say, this is not honoring the loved ones who have gone before you; this is idol worship/worshiping false gods. I don't believe this is what our ancestors wanted for us.)

After all the violence and drama surrounding my sister, I was too uncomfortable to go home, as our neighborhood felt extremely unsafe. Despite my family and heart telling me not to, I still had to work and do business. I had become engrossed with making "fast cash," but despite how hard or how much I worked business was declining fast.

After all was said and done, I concluded that God had become angry with me or, at the very least, tired of my BS.

"What have I done? What have I done so badly that I would be humbled like this? Does God's grace run out?"

I dwelled on the thought as I stood there amid my storm, searching the sky for a sign confirming this was indeed God. I scanned the area as I watched the wind rip my food setup apart for what seemed like the 100th time while every neighboring business went untouched.

"Shabriya, what are we going to do? Customers are getting angry."

"What can I do against the wind?" I shouted, annoyed by the growing line and questions.

My greed and pride led me to accept this event on top of the one God had already blessed me with. Ultimately, everything that could go wrong was going wrong. In a last ditch effort to fulfill the orders so that my customers wouldn't leave too upset, I prayed.

"Lord, is this you? I'm sorry, Lord. I repent. I beg, please have mercy on me. Please, Lord, this is too much. This event has become 100 times harder than it would normally be. Let me finish this event, and I will shut down everything and wait for you."

The wind that had been whipping me like a belt across the face, the wind that had picked up my tent with 6 people holding it down and dragged them all across the street before ripping the metal frame apart like a piece of paper, became a gentle breeze.

I finished and went to my grandmother's house. I was exhausted, yet afraid to sleep, afraid of the sleep paralysis that had been attacking me every night. Days passed, and I finally got the courage to call on God again.

"I don't know what I'm doing. Lord, I need your help." It wasn't my usual "I'm sorry, please forgive me" prayer. "I can't do this, and I desperately need you." I didn't have anything. I was afraid to go home, afraid to be alone; my whole business had been built on fear and pain, and I was afraid to even sleep.

I called on my Father, desperate for his help. Some days later, help showed up in the form of a feeling—an urgency and desire to go home that hadn't existed before.

Suddenly, I was no longer afraid of the shooting or the violence or the thought that someone might mistake me for my sister.

None of that mattered. I just needed to get home now, and so I did. I got home in record time.

I opened the door slowly, halfway expecting something to happen. I walked inside. "Now what?" I asked out loud to myself, slowly walking around the 1st floor.

Suddenly, I just knew I had to go into my "prayer room." I walked in towards the altar I had perfectly created for my ancestors when I knew I had to turn my back to it. As I did, I was met with a presence that was familiar in its heaviness, in the way it filled every molecule of the room yet somehow still exceeded the four walls that surrounded us.

This time, as I was wide awake, knowing that this wasn't just a figment of my imagination, my body fell belly down and face into the floor as if it knew what to do before I could even think of doing it. My mouth confessing before my brain could admit I was not worthy.

Guilt rushed over me, as if I had betrayed my closest friend. I did not know exactly what I had done, but somehow, I knew exactly what I had done. I wept, cried, and cried, and repented, this time not out of fear or a false sense of obligation but out of a broken heart. My heart was broken, so hurt by all the ways I had sinned against Him, yet still ignorant of how, and knowing I never wanted to do it again.

"Please show me what I've done," I pleaded, tears flowing freely in the presence of holiness that suddenly filled my prayer room. The conviction was overwhelming yet strangely specific—I knew I had sinned gravely, yet couldn't articulate exactly how. I needed divine clarity about what specifically had grieved the Holy Spirit.

"For the word of God is alive and active. Sharper than any double-edged sword, it penetrates even to dividing soul and spirit, joints and marrow; it judges the thoughts and attitudes of the heart." (Hebrews 4:12)

Immediately, my focus shifted to my Bible across the room—the same Bible that had gathered dust for years while I pursued counterfeit spirituality. It seemed to wait expectantly, glowing with an importance I couldn't explain. As I approached and lifted it with trembling hands, the pages fell open as if guided by an unseen hand, landing precisely at Acts chapter 16. This wasn't a coincidence or imagination—it was divine intervention, theologians call "the illuminating work of the Holy Spirit," making Scripture come alive with personal application.

My eyes moved across the page until one passage seemed to leap from the text literally, the words burning into my consciousness with supernatural clarity. The story described Paul's encounter with a slave girl "who had a spirit by which she predicted the future... earning a great deal of money for her owners by fortune-telling." Despite this spirit accurately identifying Paul and his companions as "servants of the Most High God," Paul recognized the demonic nature of her abilities and commanded the spirit to leave her.

The parallels to my own experience hit me with the force of divine revelation. Just like the fortune-teller I had visited, this biblical slave girl: 1) accurately predicted future events, 2) spoke truthful statements about God's servants, 3) made money through these supernatural abilities, and 4) operated through a spirit that was definitely not the Holy Spirit but a demonic entity.

"This is what I've been doing?" My heart sank to my stomach. "So, I've been doing this all through a demonic spirit? So, this isn't a gift from God," I thought.

The truth struck me like lightning—all the tarot reading, communicating with supposed ancestors, receiving seemingly accurate messages—it wasn't divine blessing but demonic deception. I felt tricked and wondered, "So what about the lady whom I went to? Is she a witch? What is going on? But she knew the Bible."

All of this because of my refusal to read the Bible for myself. After years of consuming spiritual junk food, I continued reading, hungry for truth. I turned to Matthew's Gospel, studying how Satan tempted Jesus in the wilderness, noting with growing horror how the enemy had twisted Scripture during these temptations—just as the fortune-teller had done with me. She had quoted Bible verses and spoken of God while leading me directly away from Him, a strategy as old as the Garden of Eden when the serpent asked, "Did God really say...?"

The pieces were falling into place with terrifying clarity. What I had interpreted as spiritual awakening had been a gateway to demonic influence. The "spiritual guides" and "ancestral connections" I had welcomed were the very "familiar spirits" that Scripture repeatedly condemns. The weight of this revelation pressed upon me, not with shame but with urgent clarity—I needed to completely reorient my spiritual life according to God's Word rather than subjective experiences.

I needed to get into a church community, but I did not know a single person who went to church outside of the occasional Easter or Mother's Day service. I chose to watch online.

The more I learned and studied the Bible, the harder it became to ignore how I lived.

Every time I got drunk, had premarital sex or gave into lust in any form I felt terrible. The bars and clubs I used to enjoy, now felt like prisons filled with torment. I was miserable with my life, but I wasn't ready to be the outsider again. I could not pretend I didn't know the truth. I wrestled daily and was honest with God.

"Lord, I don't know if I can do this alone." In my vulnerability, I felt like everything would be ok, that I might be "alone", but I wouldn't be lonely.

I began to tell my cousin, my closest friend. "Hey, I can't keep doing this. We're partying every weekend. It's just not sitting right in my spirit."

"I feel like I can't keep doing this," I explained again over drinks. At that point, I would have to drink so much just to silence the constant convictions of the Holy Spirit, but he was persistent, refusing to allow me to peacefully choose death now that I knew the truth.

It was time.

"Hey, cuz, I won't be able to go out and get drunk with you anymore. I'm choosing to follow God."

Confused but understanding, she said, "Ok."

"It's good if you just want to find another partner in crime," I laughed. "I just can't do it anymore."

It wasn't a complete surprise, she understood how conflicted I had been and how it was weighing on me heavy.

"Unless… You want to go on this journey with me." I felt compelled to ask, though it was not in my original plan.

She paused, looked at me, and said, "Yeah," hesitantly. Then confirmed "Yeah, let's do it."

"Are you sure?" I asked surprised by her yes. "It's not a promise that everything will be perfect. There will be ups and downs, but it will be worth it." I said, trying to give her an out now and expecting her to change her mind.

"Yes, let's do it." she repeated.

My excitement spread across my face, "Ok! Let's go."

Standing at this divine crossroads, facing the magnitude of my spiritual deception and rebellion, I finally understood what true surrender meant. I had offered God partial obedience, conditional trust, and divided loyalty all my life. Now, confronted by truth so bright it exposed every shadow, I was finally ready to let go of my flesh—my self determination, worldly desires, and spiritual compromises—and fully embrace His Spirit.

Chapter 8
Coming Home

: *The Point of No Return*

"Therefore, if anyone is in Christ, the new creation has come: The old has gone, the new is here!"- (2 Corinthians 5:17)

I had taken advantage of God's grace for years, treating it as a cosmic insurance policy rather than a transformative relationship. I had approached faith like a spiritual buffet, selecting what appealed to me while leaving behind anything that challenged my autonomy or comfort. Scripture describes this as having "a form of godliness but denying its power" (2 Timothy 3:5)—maintaining religious appearance without allowing God's power to transform my inner life.

Pride and pain had left me with a persistent desire to remain firmly planted in worldly values and pleasures. My pride told me I could define spirituality on my terms, creating a customized faith that demanded nothing I wasn't willing to give. My pain drove me toward immediate comfort rather than lasting healing, toward numbing escapes rather than transformative truth. Together, they formed a powerful coalition against genuine spiritual growth.

Deceit—both external and self-imposed—had kept me chasing empty promise after empty promise. The enemy's whispers sounded reasonable: "Your ancestors can guide you better than ancient Scripture." "This relationship might be unhealthy, but at least you're not alone." "Spiritual growth doesn't require organized religion or biblical standards." Each lie had led me further from the God who had miraculously preserved my life during my stroke, only to squander that second chance on spiritual counterfeits.

The pattern was painfully clear: I had been frantically trying to fill a God-shaped hole in my heart with incompatible substitutes—false idols, false love, attention, liquor, sex—while the very God who created that space patiently waited for me to recognize that only He could appropriately fill it. As Augustine wrote centuries ago, "Our hearts are restless until they rest in You, O Lord," my restlessness had driven me to increasingly dangerous spiritual experiments rather than divine rest.

I was deceived into believing the lie that I could repent at any time and see his kingdom. My arrogance made me think I had so much time to become holy. Like many others, I could keep putting it off, thinking that tomorrow would always come. We are being deceived with half truths, the same way Satan tried to deceive Jesus in the wilderness. Yes, "If you declare with your mouth, "Jesus is Lord," and believe in your heart that God raised him from the dead, you will be saved." (Romans 10:9 NIV) But that is only the beginning, a true relationship with the Lord will ignite a burning desire to be more like Him. Ephesians 4:23-24 instructs us to "let the Spirit renew your thoughts and attitudes. Put on your new nature, created to be like God—truly righteous and holy."

Are you like me? Believing with your heart, yet too afraid to proclaim with your lips? Are you too scared to stand out or be different from your family? Your friends? Desperately holding on to the world and the comfort you have found in the lies it provides.

Or are you the opposite, lying for all to see and hear? Proclaiming boldly with your lips, yet every day your life tells a different story? Because your heart doesn't truly believe. Living and following the world and only performing the role of a 'Christian' every Sunday?

If I stood before Jesus, would he say, "Depart from me, I never knew you?"

I asked myself after reading Matthew 7:21-23, and it was hard to admit that the answer was yes.

When Jesus conquered death through his sacrifice on the cross, he withstood pain, lies, torture, and utter humiliation that he never deserved to complete the will of his Father that we may have eternal life, and through all he endured, the worst part was when He came to this realization: "About three in the afternoon Jesus cried out in a loud voice, 'Eli, Eli, lema sabachthani?' (Matthew 27:46 NIV) (which means 'My God, my God, why have you forsaken me?')." That his Father was separated from him as he took on our sins, yet we willingly choose to separate ourselves from the Father.

Unlike Jesus, who has risen and reunited with our Father in heaven, departing from Him means death, while following Him means eternal life.

I wish I had known then what I know so clearly now: that Jesus wasn't reserved only for "church folk"—those who seemed to have their lives together, spoke the correct language, and observed the proper religious customs. He is, above all, for lost sinners exactly like me—those whose brokenness qualifies rather than disqualifies them for His grace. Perhaps this knowledge would have saved me years of heartache, prevented dangerous detours, and healed the profound loneliness that drove me toward counterfeit connections.

Finding True Peace at Last

I wish I had truly understood, not just intellectually but in the depths of my being, that "The Lord is close to the brokenhearted and saves those who are crushed in spirit" (Psalm 34:18). This isn't poetic sentiment but divine promise. The very moments when I felt most abandoned— lying in a hospital bed after my stroke, standing at the bottom of stairs my family refused to help me climb, bleeding out in the back of that clinic and facing the broken promises of relationships—were precisely when God drew nearest, when His saving power was most available, even when I couldn't perceive His presence.

If I had known I had a heavenly Father who loved and valued me unconditionally, perhaps I would have learned to love and value myself accordingly. Instead of seeking validation through others' approval, physical transformation, or romantic relationships, I might have discovered earlier the unshakable worth that comes from being cherished by the Creator of the universe. The desperate search for identity and belonging that drove so many destructive choices might have been satisfied in recognizing that I was already known completely and loved perfectly.

I wish I had known I had a savior who wanted my burdens. Maybe I wouldn't have carried them around for so long. I wish I had known I had a comforter, a healer, that I wasn't too broken for him. All he wants is our yes, our surrender, and he will take care of the rest. I wish somebody had told me back then how good God is. I wish I had known that Jesus was an option. Then I would have known peace.

Transformation is inevitable when you follow Christ Jesus. My life has been far from perfect, but I'm far from the dead woman I used to be. His word restored my hope, knowing that the good work he starts will be seen through until completion. My faith is built on the truth that Jesus died on the cross for our sins and rose three days later so that we may have eternal life.

Sister and brother, I want you to consider honestly: How long has your heart been trying to turn toward Jesus? How long has His Spirit been gently convicting you about areas of compromise, relationships that diminish rather than enhance your spiritual life, practices that provide temporary escape rather than lasting peace? How long will you run from the truth your soul recognizes, even as your mind resists it?

How long will you remain sick and tired before making the choice that changes everything? I understand the hesitation—I lived there for decades. Life is undeniably harsh; this world contains genuine evil and profound suffering. But that reality makes the good news even more urgently relevant: Jesus offers life in its fullest expression to those willing to surrender their limited versions of existence.

Seek the one who gives you life.

Jesus answered, "I am the way, the truth, and the life. No one comes to the Father except through me." John 14:6 (NIV)

Seek the one who heals. "But he was pierced for our transgressions, crushed for our iniquities; the punishment that brought us peace was on him, and by his wounds we are healed." Isaiah 53:5 (NIV)

Seek the one who gives peace beyond understanding. "And the peace of God, which transcends all understanding, will guard your hearts and minds in Christ Jesus." Philippians 4:7 (NIV)

Seek the one who redeems. "To all who mourn in Israel, he will give a crown of beauty for ashes, a joyous blessing instead of mourning, festive praise instead of despair. In their righteousness, they will be like great oaks that the Lord has planted for his glory." Isaiah 61:3 (NLT)

The End of Wandering

The peace I have been given is one that no man or money can buy, and the joy, love, peace, and freedom that Jesus has given me are available to all of you.

He is the reason why I can't turn back!

Acknowledgments

Husband

To my amazing husband, thank you for your encouragement and support. You motivated me to be obedient and share my testimony when painful memories threatened to keep me silent. Your patience and understanding sustained me through the countless hours I spent revisiting my past to bring this book to life. Your love has been a reflection of God's faithfulness in my journey. I love you.

Sam

To my esteemed editor, Samuel Adeoye, your consistent hard work and dedication have been inspiring. Your insightful suggestions and deep expertise have enhanced each page's quality and breathed life into my words, transforming them into a compelling narrative. Your commitment to excellence is evident in every detail, and I am genuinely grateful for your positive impact on my work.

Ren

To my incredible coach, Ren Lowe, I want to express my heartfelt gratitude for your support and guidance. Your encouragement to "write the book" has ignited a flame, inspiring me to share my stories and experiences with the world. Thank you for believing in my voice and empowering me to embrace my creativity.

Mom

Madré, I want you to know how much I love you. I truly appreciate everything you've done for us, always going above and beyond despite the challenges you faced. Your unwavering support means the world to me, and I am so grateful to have you by my side.

Theresa

I want to express my deepest gratitude to my beloved cousin, who holds a special place in my heart as my sister in Christ. Thank you for walking alongside me on this beautiful journey of faith and love. Your unwavering support and companionship mean the world to me.

Prayer for Readers

Lord, I thank you for the person reading this book. I trust that their desire to know you signifies that it's not too late.

I pray that your peace- the peace that surpasses understanding- the peace that calmed the stormy sea and empowered Peter to step out in faith—washes over them. As they seek comfort in their healing and trauma, may they find it in you, the ultimate comforter. Let your presence meet them where they are and be felt by all around them.

I pray that they will turn away from worldly emptiness that leads to death and instead embrace the eternal life that comes from accepting Jesus as Lord and Savior. May your life-giving word be within reach every time they are in need.

I pray, dear reader, that you will come and lay your burdens down, seeking to be filled by His Holy Spirit rather than the things of this world. Trust Him, for He will give you beauty for your ashes, and allow Him to become your firm foundation.

In Jesus' name,

Amen

Discussion Questions

For Book Clubs and Bible Studies

1. **Spiritual Displacement**: Shabriya describes the Fillmore district and her life as experiencing "spiritual displacement." How do you see this theme developing throughout her story? Have you ever experienced a sense of spiritual displacement in your own life?

2. **Divine Timing**: Throughout the memoir, God's interventions often come at the last moment. What instances stood out to you, and why do you think God sometimes waits until we've reached our breaking point before revealing His presence?

3. **The Nature of Suffering**: When Shabriya asks God, "Why me?" during her stroke, He responds, "Why not?" How does this exchange challenge conventional understandings of suffering? What does Scripture teach us about why believers face hardships?

4. **Family Wounds**: Shabriya's relationship with her mother leaves deep wounds that affect her entire life. How does her eventual understanding and forgiveness of her mother reflect Christ's teachings about forgiveness? What family wounds have you had to bring before God?

5. **The Veil Between Worlds**: During her near-death experience, Shabriya experiences a thinning of the veil between physical and spiritual realities. How did this experience change her understanding of life, death, and eternity? How does Scripture describe the relationship between the seen and unseen realms?

6. **Human vs. Divine Love**: After experiencing divine love during her coma, Shabriya returns to find human love painfully conditional and limited. How does Scripture differentiate between human and divine love? How can Christians better reflect God's unconditional love to others?

7. **False Comforts**: Tequila, romantic relationships, physical transformation—Shabriya turns to many false comforts before finding true peace in Christ. What false comforts have you turned to in your own life? What makes these compelling, even when we know they won't satisfy?

8. **Spiritual Warfare**: Shabriya describes hearing a voice telling her to kill herself and feeling a presence breathing on her neck. How does her experience align with Scriptural descriptions of spiritual warfare? How can believers prepare themselves for such battles?

9. **Physical vs. Spiritual Identity**: Shabriya's obsession with her appearance nearly costs her life during the BBL surgery. How does her journey illustrate the dangers of finding identity in physical appearance? What does Scripture teach about our true identity?

10. **Ancestral Worship**: The author describes how she turned to ancestral worship, finding it more comforting than turning to God. What made this practice so appealing to her? How does Scripture address the human tendency to create spiritual practices that feel more accessible than a direct relationship with God?

11. **The Strong Black Woman Stereotype**: Shabriya notes how the "strong Black woman" trope prevented her from getting her needed help. How can churches better support those who feel pressure to be strong for everyone else? How does Christ's

example of vulnerability challenge cultural expectations of strength?

12. **Turning Points**: What is the most significant turning point in Shabriya's spiritual journey? Was there a moment that particularly moved or challenged you? Why?

13. **Testing the Spirits**: When Shabriya finally begins reading her Bible, she discovers that many of her "spiritual" experiences were deceptive. What guidance does 1 John 4:1 offer for discerning true and false spiritual experiences? How can believers develop this discernment?

14. **The Hospital as Metaphor**: The author moves from physical hospitals to spiritual healing. How does her experience of physical healing parallel her spiritual journey? What similarities do you see between medical treatment and spiritual transformation?

15. **Cannot Turn Back**: "I Can't Turn Back" refers to Shabriya's commitment to follow Christ regardless of the cost. What does it mean practically to reach a point of no return in one's faith journey? Have you experienced such a moment?

Personal Reflection Questions

1. Shabriya's experiences with medical professionals and family members often left her feeling unheard and invalidated. When have you felt similarly invisible? How did that experience affect your relationship with God?

2. The author describes how God used her rejection by others to create a deeper dependence on Him. How

has God used painful experiences in your life to draw you closer to Him?

3. What aspect of Shabriya's spiritual journey do you most identify with? Which parts challenge you the most?

4. Near the end of her story, Shabriya writes, "I wish I had known then what I know so clearly now: that Jesus wasn't reserved only for 'church folk'..." What misconceptions about faith have stood between you and a deeper relationship with Christ?

5. Shabriya's transformation required her to let go of false identities, destructive coping mechanisms, and spiritual counterfeits. What might God be asking you to release to experience the freedom Shabriya ultimately found?

Recommended books

➤ Spiritual growth Bible NLT
➤ Holy Bible ESV
➤ *Discerning the Voice of God* by Priscilla Shirer
➤ *Habits of the Household: Practicing the Story of God in Everyday Family Rhythms* -by Justin Whitmel Earley
➤ *Exercising Spiritual Authority* - by Mike Connell
➤ *Gay Girl Good God* - by Jackie Hill Perry
➤ *Welcome to the basement* - by Tim Ross
➤ *How to Tell the Truth: The Story of How God Saved Me to Win Hearts--Not Just Arguments*- by Preston Perry
➤ *Crazy Faith: It's Only Crazy Until It Happens* by Michael Todd

Resources for readers

Mental health services

If you or someone you know needs emotional support, contact (Call or text) the national mental health hotline: 988.

Free/affordable therapy at www.growtherapy.com

https://openpathcollective.org/

Federally qualified health centers nationwide provide mental health services, and many offer tele-counseling. They will help you even if you have no health insurance; you pay what you can afford based on your income

Domestic violence- National Domestic Violence Hotline

Call 1.800.799.SAFE (7233)

Text "START" to 88788

Chat & Resources www.thehotline.org

- Substance abuse www.findtreatment.gov/

- 988 Suicide and Crisis Lifeline. Call or text 988

- Trafficking -National Human Trafficking Hotline

Call 888-373-7888. Text INFO to 233733
humantraffickinghotline.org

About the Author

Shabriya Hill is a wife, mother, writer, speaker, food entrepreneur and survivor whose life was forever changed by a near fatal stroke at the age of 24. Through her raw and powerful storytelling, she shares her journey from trauma and abandonment to healing, faith, and divine transformation.

A native of San Francisco historic Fillmore District Shabriya is passionate about empowering others to believe in the possibility of redemption no matter how broken their past.

When she felt called to write, she was unsure yet obedient. With no "formal" training and a recent desire to become an author, she stepped out in faith. Inspired by the Lord's transformative work in her own life, Shabriya now shares stories of hope, restoration, and God's unfailing love.

She currently has multiple publications in progress, all with the sole purpose of advancing the kingdom by encouraging the "lost" to come back to Christ so they, too, may receive the same peace and freedom she now enjoys.

Her debut memoir, *I CAN'T TURN BACK*— is a bold and inspiring testimony of survival, surrender, and the God who makes all things new.

Connect with the Author

Website – OnaHillPublishing.com

Email - Shabriya.HillO@gmail.com |
Coordinator@OnaHillPublishing.com

Tiktok - shabriyahill.o

Linkedin - Shabriya Hill-O

Facebook - Shabriya Hill

Instagram - Shabriya_O

Epilogue

I stood there, feeling relief and hope—I'm redeemed! But now what? For most of my life, I had been at ease with Jesus as my savior, savoring His gift of grace. Yet, for the first time, I felt a stirring deep within me—a longing to know Him as my savior and the faithful Lord of my life.

With a heart full of anticipation, I reached for my Bible and whispered a prayer: "Lord, I'm stepping into the unknown. I might not have all the answers, but I trust you. Please let your desires become my desires. Amen."

After studying Matthew, I was inspired to fast, deny my flesh, nourish my spirit daily, and grow in wisdom and knowledge of God's word. God began to reveal secrets through dreams and visions. What I once thought was guidance from ancestors, I now recognize as God's voice speaking to me.

When I received a dream warning me of the loss of someone close, I felt a surge of urgency. I implored my family members to turn their lives around and embrace Jesus. Though they viewed my concerns skeptically, I poured out my heart, urging them to change their ways. I did not know who we would lose or when, but I was overcome with an undeniable sense that death was approaching.

As I came to the end of my fast, I took a moment to focus on forgiveness for those who are closest to me. In the way that Colossians 3:13 instructs us to "Make allowance for each other's faults and forgive anyone who offends you. Remember, the Lord forgave you, so you must forgive others."

I didn't want to dwell on the past or rehash old wounds; this journey was my own, not for their sake but for my healing. In that space of reflection, I sought to forgive and release the burdens I had been carrying. The Lord extended His forgiveness to me, and it struck me deeply. I realized I hadn't done anything to deserve it—no actions to earn such grace. Yet, He offered it freely. In that moment, I learned that forgiveness isn't about worthiness; it's a beautiful gift that reminds us of the boundless nature of love and mercy. He made me understand that forgiveness is a precious gift to be given freely. My heart, once hardened like stone, had softened like tender flesh. My burden was lifted, and the chains bound to me finally broke. Embracing forgiveness has truly set me free.

After months of silence, I finally reached out to my brother, hoping to find forgiveness between us. Reflecting on our past interactions, I recognized that I hadn't approached him with the care he deserved. Fear and panic often guided my actions, making me try to push him to change without truly understanding his perspective. It dawned on me that Jesus showed me the importance of leading with empathy.

While my concerns for him were genuine and his soul truly needed saving, I realized that my delivery didn't embody the compassion Jesus calls us to show one another. Thankfully, we were able to reconcile our differences. I'm genuinely grateful to God for allowing me to have that meaningful conversation with my baby brother, especially knowing it would be one of our last.

As I woke up that morning, a deep, unsettling pain settled in the pit of my stomach, and I couldn't shake the worry that I might be falling ill again. My stomach churned with anxiety, and my mind raced with uncertainty. This feeling was unlike anything I had experienced before. I tried to lie back down in a last-ditch effort to quiet the turmoil.

A couple of hours later, my phone rang—it was my mom. "Good morning!" she greeted, and I couldn't help but smile at her cheerful tone. "How are you?" she asked, concern evident. I hesitated, knowing I had to be truthful, yet uncertain how to explain. "I'm feeling some stomach issues, but I can't quite figure it out. I don't know what's happening; I think I'll lie down for now."

She was navigating through traffic on her way home. We shared a few laughs, which momentarily lifted my spirits. "Hold on," she said suddenly, "I'll call you back." I waited eagerly, looking forward to her return call. When the phone rang again, I answered with my usual "Madré!" But instead of lighthearted conversation, I was met with a heart wrenching screech as my brother's name was yelled in panic, piercing through my discomfort and leaving me to brace for what was about to unfold.

What am I going to do? She cried out, "Mom, Mom!" Panic filled my voice. "What happened?!" I begged. My mom had just received a call that my brother had been shot, and he was being rushed to the hospital. In that moment, tears began to spill down my cheeks. I quickly put on whatever clothes I could find, fighting against the overwhelming fear that gripped me. I silently prayed, "Lord, no! Please, please protect my brother. Let him be okay." I told my mom I would meet her there, and I reached out to my sister so she could join us. As I woke my daughter, I gently asked her to get dressed, trying to remain strong for her while my heart ached for my brother.

My mom called back, her voice rising in panic. "Shabriya, no, no!" she shouted repeatedly, each word laced with desperation. I felt the urgency in her tone and couldn't help but scream back, "No, no, no! I'm on my way!" Determination kicked in as I prepared to rush to her side.

As I stood waiting for the Lyft driver to arrive, I fought to project an air of calm for my daughter, desperately trying to shield her from the tumultuous storm brewing within me. I wanted to be the pillar of strength she needed, but my resolve began to wane with each passing moment. No, no, no—please, not now. A profound, unsettling feeling settled deep in my spirit, whispering that my brother was gone.

The pain washed over me like a tidal wave, heavy and suffocating, an urgent weight that pressed down upon my heart. Yet, a stubborn part of me clung to hope, unwilling to fully embrace the reality before me. The ten-minute ride to the hospital stretched into what felt like an eternity, each second dragging on as if time itself was reluctantly prolonging my agony.

Upon arriving, I was met by the haunting sight of our family huddled together outside the hospital. Their collective grief was palpable, echoing like a mournful symphony in the air. My little sister's scream pierced through the silence, a raw expression of anguish that sent shivers down my spine. I could gauge the devastating truth from their expressions—their eyes had an unmistakable emptiness; he was no longer with us.

Defeat hung heavily in the air, an invisible shroud that draped over my family. When I laid eyes on my mom, the sight shattered my already fragile heart into a billion more pieces. The gut-wrenching pain etched across her face was more than I could bear, a visceral reminder of how deeply this loss cut through us all. At that moment, I struggled to comprehend how it could feel any worse.

I began to pray for a miracle, fully aware that I serve a God capable of all things—the same God who raised Lazarus from the dead. I prayed relentlessly, yet my reality remained unchanged.

As I stood inside the hospital, the truth hit me hard: this was real life, and I had to confront it. I felt lost and turned to prayer, but all that came out was, "God, why?" I could not comprehend how God could permit this to happen.

I had been devoted to prayer, having just completed a 21day fast and immersed myself in scripture. My brother and I had finally started communicating again after months of silence. So why? Why would you take him from me?

My sadness morphed into anger, and I directed that anger toward God. It was a struggle I wasn't ready for, and I needed answers.

I pulled myself up from the puddle of tears that had become my makeshift bed, staring up at the ceiling as an anguished scream escaped my lips. "Lord, Your Word promises that you are near to the brokenhearted and those crushed in spirit!" I cried; my voice laced with desperation. "But my heart feels shattered, and my spirit is beyond repair—where are You in all this?" My tone was filled with accusation, as if His promises had somehow missed me in my despair.

Eventually, exhaustion took over, and I surrendered to a deep sleep, a temporary escape from the weight of my pain.

But God had other plans.